TEAR HERE

– – – –

TEAR HERE

— — — —

Words, and a few drawings, by
ROBERT TEAR

ANDRE DEUTSCH

First published 1990 by
André Deutsch Limited
105-106 Great Russell Street
London WC1B 3LJ

ISBN 0 233 98572 3

Printed in Great Britain by
St Edmundsbury Press
Bury St Edmunds, Suffolk

To Hilly, Becky and Lizzie

1

I had made a mistake. At an inexpensive shoe-shop in King Street, Hammersmith, I had bought a pair of DM's, or Doctor Martin's to those who are not so conversant with the terminology of early punk. These boots are seamless and ugly and look like bull terriers. The uppers rest on contained beds of air in soles thick but light with deep treads. Nothing wrong with all this, one might say. I would readily agree, had the size been right. Sadly it was not. 'At least half a size too small,' my feet whispered, but I wouldn't hear them and was now paying in full for my impatience. Blistered a lot, bleeding a little, I scuttled slowly like a defeated crab through the rain and wind down, or was it up, a street in Paris.

It's mid-afternoon. The pavements are too narrow, especially for the French; the buildings St Germain way, reflective, grey, intuitive, bursting with history. Stumbling further I see a brown bilious Seine heaving its way past its ever-rebuilt crossings.

Nothing special in all this. Absolutely nothing. Nothing other than my mind and feet and I suppose my body was encircled with a thick mist of fear. I could see everything and nothing. I was seeing clearly, with blind eyes.

'The cause of this vaporous panic?'

'Me! What other cause can there be?'

'Well!'

'It's me but not me, in a strange way.'

You see, a singer is always me and loves to be so, but the thing that occupies his throat is the *not* me, is THE VOICE. This free agent has few debts to pay but rests uneasy. It stays free of rent or gratitude. It behaves well some of the time, it can delight at others, but still it remains if certainly never a foe, at all times a circumspect, dangerous, loving, angelic, never-to-be-taken-for-granted agent, like an intelligent wife and a true friend. But also (and this is the peak of verity, when flying easily in good times from chestnut to poplar) never me.

Here is the fatal flaw, and here I feel I should begin this untidy, slippy, crooked and excited path of a singer who can see (at least as far as his temperament allows).

The explanation of my blind panic was that at the Paris Opera that same evening I had a performance of *Salomé* by Richard Strauss. Under normal circumstances the tenant of my *gorge*, with its tiny but tough arms, is fair and kind. This is perhaps an exaggeration but to expect less would be foolhardy and I don't want it to hear. This day, a March one I think, was an off. Prickly needles for days had seeded themselves in the back of the upper palate that teasing distance behind the nose. I understand perfectly that these bug colonies must breed and multiply and at times must use me as their maternity ward, but I have never understood their timing.

Would they seriously group and congeal around those light tendons and stop the touching? Why such a vulnerable spot? Why not lower down with the chance of septuple pneumonia? Anything would be better than this. Such thoughts bring a paranoia complete. The world is now nothing but me, no less than this, but also more. The world is now nothing but the Voice. Every slight change in heat is now meticulously recorded.

'I know it's shifting down.'

'Oh God, another centimetre.'

'What then?'

'Yes, it's on its way.'

'What about tonight?'

'Oh, let's brave it out.'

'Trust your technique!'

'But that's no good with this going on.'

'What *do* we do, then?'

What do I do. The person changes. Mark this well, the attack is abating for a while. The Voice is now being forced back into me and me around it. The philosophical unity is becoming a reality. That hand picking my nose is mine. It does not have a separate existence. That mind thinking unspeakable thoughts is mine. That voice about to hand me a hiding is me.

What happens of course depends logically on the degree of infection or madness. In the case above everything passed smoothly by with passages clear, thoughts and attitudes neat. That this need not be the case I will explain, but not now.

Such is the madness that affects many singers. I cannot speak for any other than myself, but from my now extensive experience I conclude that the previous history is in no way unique. To enquire deeper into this prevailing madness of insecurity might be of interest, but before embarking on this philosophical, psychological saga, perhaps it would be entertaining to ask why some people feel the ungovernable necessity to sing. It is an ought?

Why then sing at all? Why complicate what might be an easy life with such an ineffable?

2

In my case, the cause of the rot was the evil apple that was my grandfather. A ship's blacksmith by trade, thinker *manqué* and dandy by *gout*, solitary by temperament, he sang for all these reasons as an amateur and was complimented by the high professionals of his day (Ben Davis for one) and had to choose between a tiedmanship to Arsenal (football) or Bailey's (docks); the latter being more secure, the seeming defter arts of foot-touch and voice-touch were forgotten; but he made many 'renaissance' pokers and for that I am doubly grateful.

However, seeds once sown in a willing soil will flourish, water at a pinch. For my case I must say it was ploughed and tilled. At an early innocence I had held my position as a useful chorister in the church of St Mary, Barry, Glamorgan, later (because of Masonic differences, my father hating the brethren) of St Paul, but more importantly as the boy mascot of the Barry Ladies' Choir. Christopher Robin (the song) never knew such indulgence, at least for thirty years, but that's another bit.

This does not explain the obsession with singing that was to develop. If Wales is your homeland, the chances were in those distant days that you would be (in order of public esteem) a doctor, a teacher, a good sportsman-teacher-doctor, a singer or a boxer (not in our house, son). The tradition of choir singing with much sentiment and little discipline was well to the fore in Welsh culture. However, I must not mislead you. The choirs in which I sang would not have been seen dead nibbling on *Bread of Heaven* or cooking fried eggs in *Sospan Fach*. No, my church choirs communed with super English composers like Stanford and Walmsley. I remember with glee the choirboys' corruption of

Alcock in B flat into something far richer. The nod we often threw to Tomkins, who as organist of St David's Pembroke salved a little our national leanings. Nevertheless, however and whatever was sung one thing was clear, singing was not considered as the dubious womb of perverts and ponces but was part of a living art. At least the obsession was not artificially discouraged. I then went to the local grammar school where a music master with beady hawk eye, a certain A. S. Brinn, spotted my talent – shifted me to Cambridge, the source of all self-pleasurable things, and thence through the cheerful and generous hands of the loyal David Valentine Willcocks to the more careless hands of God at St Paul's Cathedral and finally (at least in formative terms) to the butterfingers of Benjamin Britten. In his defence let me immediately say that a wilful piece of butter is a tricky object to lay paws on. All these comments may seem cynical and ungrateful, but I assure you they're not. They all stand on the teetering threshold of a life-story. The influences live on in feebly remembered ways as all the past does. It changes imperceptibly yet constantly to confuse: it is only a shadow of the very events, it appears like a falling leaf before our only too willingly beguiled eyes. The threshold we stand on continues to tremble because it is an illusion.

3

I have found that my colleagues, with a few exceptions, come from – for want of a better term – the working class. This generality does not confine itself to the United Kingdom but can be seen world-wide. Having attempted to analyse this fact in my own case, I think I should assume the mantle of the social historian (red and black naturally, what other colours would conjurors use?) and assert (this is a very impressive word) that singers tend to arise from the lower strata of society because not only is it not a despicable activity as discussed previously but also it could be a path to freedom. As Alberich says in *Das Rheingold*, *'Bin ich nun frei?'* (Am I now free?) The answer might be for the bored intelligent, the shackled breathing stifling second-class air, abiding in a town conceived by sightless men, 'When I sing, *"Ja, wirklich frei"*.' (Yes, truly free.) The possibilities of such freedom would need a book of a different nature from this for its discussion. But let us for this life-tick consider the loss of talent from the other strata of our society. I think especially of those grand denizens of the garden party, hunt ball and crowded cocktail room, the natural masters of our ring who with effortless ease peel a lemon of its rind at forty paces through a seething room and at ten could make the flaying of Titian appear a bagatelle. Such natural placing of the voice, such authority of utterance hints at careers that would have left Caruso a castrato and Sutherland a semaphore.

Such fantasy suitably stabled, the question of the general nature of singers arises. As I write these words I realise with even more intensity the idiocy of speech. Not only are words infinitely misunderstandable but infinitely dumb. This is a hobby-horse of mine which is not as wooden as it might appear and has within its belly, at the crack of a whip, the ability to turn into the nag death so freezingly bestrides. I will for the moment put these questions in the stall and assert that all singers do indeed have a general nature. It is one of openness, generosity, pride, vulnerability and – dare I say it – innocence. All begin so and change with success or lack of it. Having been thus branded, I believe they can then be categorised in three. The first, the intensely successful and seriously rich; the second, the neat, comfortable and successful; and thirdly the group without the first two.

4

Concerning the first. They begin as the others but change with the mark of Nosferatu, Count Alucard or fame. This might appear to be a gratuitous piece of exaggeration, were it not for the fact that the objects of this truth lie yawlingly under our scope. The brilliant tenor, that voice of a generation, that sweet boy with generous gift, that dear putto is found to have a voice of unusual worth and communication. Such a gift is received, not before its time, because time is always a collaborator, into the eager rectangular breasts of the rich and greedy. 'How many hours under the knife?' 'Don't speak of it.' From this moment the Farinelli of our time becomes public property. This international Voice is now sucked-upon or chewed at will, rather as Freia's golden apples were consumed under a cloudless heaven (to sustain the prevailing opera). The innocent boy, now stripped, forgets his impulse, ignores his *'raison'* (which was the honest occupation of his talent) and becomes the plaything of the soulless gods. It was remarked by Alan Cunningham in his *British Painters* of 1830 that the whole of Hogarth's *oeuvre* could be outsold in one night by the fee of Farinelli because of his patronage. Such is the power of the very gifted to the very rich. There is, however, an obverse equation (not that it is of any importance except to this gnarled watcher), this being, the more the singer becomes the plaything of the heartless gods, the more he loses his relevance to his colleagues and his conductor. Thus: the star becomes encumbered with 'staritude' (this word might be made clear in the next Oxford dictionary as 'the inability to see past the self with its baubles and trinkets, the inability to learn even as the faculty was there, and as the infinite power of delusion.' This assumes that the writer cannot suffer a similar fate. He can and might for this is the fate of much of humanity. The delusion of the superstar bars him from communication with his fellows, he makes vain passes at bonhomie but is defeated by his success. He is finally also barred from himself, because the fawning, mendacious mob convince him he is a different man. Having been born an *homme ordinaire*, he is unduly teased by success. The world of goodies corrupts unduly as both Wotan and Don Giovanni would testify. The itch of fame corrupts utterly. The super-rich singer will be seen as a second-rate brain, colleague and person. His frailty lies in his vulnerability. He believes his power *is* power, he needs his goodies again and again. He becomes a victim to be consumed by his public. He will inject cortisone to survive night following night,

but will die. The public in their guilt will then mourn their martyr, build shrines and worship the one who believed them too much.

5

Concerning the second. A small précis now for those who have just walked into a bookshop to escape the rain and have opened this book at this page. The nature of singers and singers' natures is being discussed. The super-successful have been parked, the ordinary successful are now put into gear. Here a closer knot of angels cannot be perceived. The testing medieval quizzler of how many angels can occupy the head of pin is here answered: it is, as many as the kind colleagues that I have had the pleasure to work with over the past twenty-eight years. Although socialising (what a peach of a word) with singers outside the stage or platform is unusual, the camaraderie is endless within these confines. I will tell you why.

When a singer chirps there is a finality of utterance which cannot be denied. While other artists can strike out or overpaint and conductors can hope that no one has noticed (always in vain, let me say), the singer at that one single moment is judged – every moment a final judgement. Here there is no room to apologise or claw indulgence. If you split a note, if you knocked one down, it will have been well noted by public and critics.

It is comforting to group the various watchers together as collectively inimical to us. We, of course, depend on their support when watching our antics, but they choose to come and pay to do so. My temperament finds the approbation of the curtain call elementally tedious. For me there is nothing better than a quick removal of make-up (if I was unlucky enough to have it forced on me) and a *'schlüpfe denn Heim'* (slip away home) and 'through a *schwefelkluft'* (cleft in the rock) if necessary. These days there seems to be an increasing desire in the audience for participation. In some symbiotic way they feel that they are transported to the stage and that a performing or vocal role is in some way laid upon them; a kind of 'beam me up Countess'. I would wish to nail this growing bogy. It is true that in many ways our relationship is symbiotic, but they pays their moneys and they takes their chances. There can be no guaranteed satisfaction on this wheel.

Now I come to consider it, the role of the singer does feel uncommonly chancy, rather like roulette, but I think that Russian roulette would be nearer the mark.

A technique under most circumstances will see us through but there are some (sometimes of our own vaunting faults, sometimes fatefully thrown) when it won't. When the not arrives all the dissimilar people occupying a similar work, will unite; life lines are chucked, missed and chucked again, boats are launched but the breakers still break. The job is so difficult and is accepted as such by the trade, that there is little room for gloating or self love. One night a lion, the next a dog. Natural solidarity becomes the name of the game. Now back on land, it is so difficult for any agent to break or bypass this thorny unity. The director who tries soon finds himself in the prickly brakes, as does the conductor. We know what can be done, they hope to convince us of their dreams. When the dreams are flown on rainbow wings we are immensely fulfilled. But much of the time we are not convinced and must needs convince ourselves that the effort we put out is worth it. We may not believe that we are part of a dud, for should we, in that blink creation becomes impossible.

We all know the important rehearsals and feel a tension not unlike that of the athlete. We know that a first piano rehearsal with a conductor is crucial. All his opinions crystallise at this moment and an unfavourable impression will remain for the rest of the run. We feel that at the first 'stage and orchestra' rehearsal we must forget virtually all that we had learned of the production and concentrate entirely on the conductor. Watch and keep watching. Do not get behind. We understand that the greatest benefit we can give to a conductor is being no trouble. When he has eighty or so musicians in front of him, many of whom do not wish to be there, he doesn't need extra anxiety and worry over his singers. We all know these things, we share these bonds. So all in all, a salt of the earth confederation, and like all such groups, full of all types from the fearfully dull to the super intelligent. All sorts rest between, especially those who believe they are the last but are in fact the first. The humour of singers is notoriously broad, not to say vile, but it is shared by virtually all and seems to me to be a way out of the extreme tension which we know will occur the moment we step into the lights. Those who think Mozart juvenile because of his scatological trait, beware opera dressing-rooms.

6

Now for the worm in the rose, the canker in the bud. Category three. I beg you now to imagine your most blessed day. 'Go on now, anything considered, yes, anything.' While you are thinking, I will tell you mine. I wake early and kiss my girl's (Hilary's) little white ears without hardly waking her and in seconds bedeck myself in vicious green. The shirt and the shorts don't quite match but are near enough to disturb eye instantly followed by gut. I then lollop to the tennis courts right in front of our house. (They are public ones, but this I can only admit under bamboo ticklings.) Here on these very courts, and on this one theatrical court covered with twigs and droppings, I will give my opponent a larruping, my shots so fast, the skin peels from the ball like curdled milk. I return, by this time Hilly is up and we decide to go to town. With pockets awash we get out of our taxi at Bond Street. We visit some friends (those barrow-boys in suits, that organise the trade in other people's talents), namely the art dealers. Individually they are amusing, kind, sweet and often generous. We walk on to a famous auctioneer's where, as we indolently lean on a counter, some poor bugger from the street arrives, under his arm a brown, tattered package. He braves the contemptuous and icy stare of the English goddess (Santa Henrietta) behind the counter on which we lean. The building, once a rather intimate and dog-eared place, has recently been whored-up to represent nothing less than the get of an ocean liner and a global hotel. International business is the word. Our poor man being deracinated, asks waveringly for his package to be opened and commented on. He eventually unties it and presents it to the bespectacled eyes of a pimply toff, newly out of nappies. The offended gaze of the runt sends the man scuttling (in a similar style to me that day in Paris), his package not even resecured. I follow him into the street (Hilly behind to avoid any possible ensuing shame), commiserate on his heinous treatment and ask him the nature of his package. He shows it to me. I see an unknown illustration from Blake's *Job* series. Now not only do the sons of the morning shout, but so do I. We send the shivering sprite to those who will with him fairly deal and proceed to a fish lunch, where with genteel art we tear the creature from its bones and divide a wine that could not satisfy a thirsty man.

It must be something to do with the air in this area. The man who serves us is like the twin of the one at the auction house. The attitudes are so similar as to be almost the same. Haughty, short-sighted, infinitely bored, contemptuous, hubristic, arrogant would be six ways of describing him. Anyway, it's the first Wednesday in June, Derby day. We have a three-legged nag that is running. We scream to the course (what an unattractive place!) and arrive to see him fall over a placard proclaiming some rights or other and immediately confined to the glue pot. *Sic transit gloria mundi*, ashes to ashes, horses for gods, No I mean dogs. I ring my mate David Barrie at the Cabinet Office and discuss the similarities of the Lao-Tse and Eckhart or of a Ruskin and a Leonardo drawing. By the way, we are back home now (opposite the tennis courts, remember), my two daughters Becky and Liz are there and fearing that I won't get much of a look in when the three women get gassing, I nip up the stairs, sit in a beautiful blue room and write a masterpiece in seven lines – it encompasses with puerile ease the wisdom of time, the imagination of Shakespeare, the gall of

Eliot, the touch tenderness of Dickinson, the wings of
Milton, the godly landscape of Traherne, to mention
but six. Having given birth with contemptuous ease
to genius, I try again and prove conclusively that all
politicians live in a spiritual wilderness and that their
feeble efforts of control are mute nods in the direction of a God they cannot admit. Such overwhelming
success reddens my cheeks. The sense of colour now
awakened, I spring to paint. With a couple of languid
strokes I convey the secret and pathos of life. God
was even more me at this moment than ever before.
We now 'paint the sky with *our* careless hands'. Such
blood-raisin' moments now gone, a spot of golden tarn
helm special brew soothes the nerves. (I forgot to mention earlier that the rather pretentious phone call I had
earlier with my pal did also chance upon the merits of
bitter. Fuller's contra Young's is always good for ten
minutes' intellectual haggling.) 'Tele' the *Somnus de nos
jours*, claims a minute or two of attention, then with a
final burst of activity (perhaps the white ears kissed
the while) the *Somnus de tous jours* clubs me. By the
way, I forgot to mention that the forgotten Blake is
of Job offering an oblation before his children. I think
Hannah Palmer might have copied it.

'I can see by your face that you haven't completed
your perfect day, yet.'

'I'll give you a moment more.'

'I'll tell you what Caruso did for exercise.'

Caruso: 'A singer's life is such an active one, with

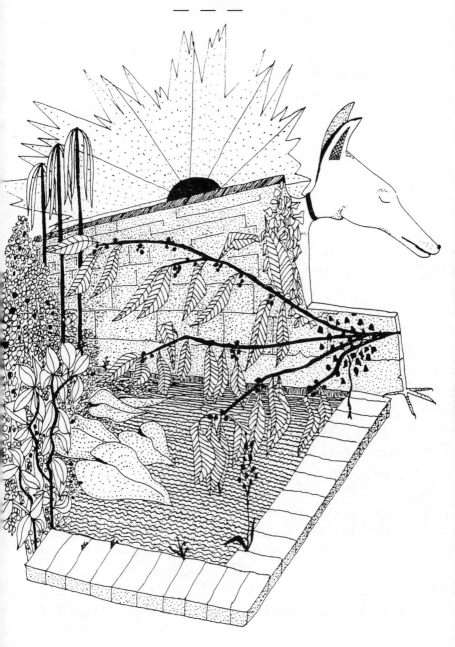

19

rehearsals and performances, that not much opportu-
nity is given for exercise, and the time to do this must,
of course, be governed by individual needs. I find a few
simple physical exercises in the morning after rising,
somewhat similar to those practised in the Army, or
the use for a few minutes of a pair of light dumbbells
very beneficial. Otherwise I must content myself with
an occasional automobile ride.' (Extract from Caruso's
autobiography, now long out of print and rare.)

7

'Good, I see you've finished at last.'

Well, this is where the worm nibbles contentedly
away, right in the heart of the heart. Those of category
three, the unsuccessful singers all hold a similar vision
but it rests within the delusory drug of the Voice. Can
you imagine that moment when the throat opens (in
Caruso's terms) and you stand a Zeus of expression?
Can you believe the physical frisson that attends a
note perfectly placed, an eighth of an inch behind
the front teeth, rib-cage up, column of air perfectly
supported and the voice on top like a table-tennis ball
on a fountain of water at the fun fair? Well, if you
can't let me assure you that alcohol, amphetamines,

the spirit of the soul, will give you nothing like it. The grey ordinary day turns into a physical and spiritual Valhalla with no St Peter demanding credentials. (I *do* know that St Peter probably never spent much time with Mr and Mrs Fricka-Wotan, but you must know what I mean.) The drug of singing is a cruel master – it will confuse – it will always say, 'I wasn't at my best' – 'That person hated my person' – 'They can't see what I have.' It will always be the same as in all addictions, it is always everybody's fault, but never mine. The world can seem a cruel place but it is wisdom to know that God is not a social worker and that true health lies within. As Tippett says (after Jung, I think), 'I would know my shadow and my light, so shall I at last be whole.' Those who do not have the gift in enough quantity and shapes had better acquaint themselves with the fact and soon, lest promising lives be left in the shambles of ruin and despair.

8

'If singing is not just a natural vocal gift, I pray you, tell me what it is?'

'It is, dear sir, the most complex equation known to man, the extraordinary outcome of silvered cross-hatchings on a white base mixed with club-footed thunderings and diplomatic cunning, with truth, a small touch of gift, sharpened antennae and pricked ears, Donnerings, logic, tooings and Frohings' . . .

'Please, do stop! Tell me plainly, so that I can get on with my toast.'

I made a suitable pause, no, a weighty pause, while the atoms of toast chirped, flew and played unopposed and said . . .

'It is forty per cent talent, the rest a combination of intangibles. These last concern themselves very great-ly with the co-habitation of person with personality. It requires quiet intuition and wit, it requires, shortly, those same qualities which make a man most at home in the world.'

What I was saying of course, was that if a person of influence likes you, and you do your tasks well, he will continue to employ you. I did forget to tell my munching friend, however, that a deal of study is entailed in getting up a competent technique and a great deal of barefaced arrogance in order to ignore the second-hand, mediocre advice that at the start is thrust on you from all around.

This last point cannot be too highly stressed for in it, for me at least, lies the true source of power. One's own intuition must at all times be paramount and trusted.

9

I will now be serious for the next few pages. In them I will try to convey how a certain philosophy can at once liberate the soul and at the same time distance it so that your tasks often appear ludicrous. There can be no doubt that one's soul is changed by one's beliefs, as is one's face. The soul thus changed, one's vision of work, the world and all things immaterial likewise is altered. Please bear with me.

'Have some more toast.'

The problem is, we are born so egocentric that we are as far removed from the spirit of Love as possible (hence the Catholic doctrine of original sin). All babies yearn for instant bodily satisfaction (quite properly as they must survive), every need must be gratified. Many people remain in this stage, but that is getting far ahead of the argument. As this infantile stage slowly loses power, the self gradually begins to feel uneasy, sensing a growing emptiness; the self senses an insecurity and hops into the vacuum. The agile but often lying mind, being part of nature, cannot

23

abide this state and seeks at first worryingly and then hectically for something to fill it. It decides that first it should build a high wall and then fill the most of itself with concepts of achievement and winning. The bits of itself that object at this stage, the mind packs away in a darkened upstairs room. Now this strange action can keep mind and body occupied for quite a long time, because the resultant concoction of acceptable, secure self has a wonderful coating of chocolate and a filling of fudge which is indeed very tasty. It will of course finally be seen as the lie it is, and then die, probably by self-consumption, a kind of chewy suicide. But having started on the great course of false action the habitualised, security-conscious mind can conceive of nothing outside itself that doesn't bring pain with it. So it puts worries up at the top of the house in another dark room quite close to that unacceptable bit of the brain. But having done this, it becomes sad and lightly guilty because it feels something is wrong. Sometimes the sadness becomes so unbearable and the desire for security and control so great that the obvious fact it cannot exist drives the sufferer to kill himself, thus at least procuring security and control in some devious, dubious way.

Now if from the moment of birth we were taught that there can be no security and that all success or achievement is merely what you think it is, what a realistic world might be formed.

I am sometimes asked, 'What is the point of life?'

This question is often engendered by my assertion that there may be no personal afterlife. I hasten to add that I have no way of knowing, but my intuition leads me in this direction. The question makes two fundamentally wrong suggestions, to my mind. The first of these, that there should be a point, the second that there must be eternity in order to round it off neatly and securely for us. The thought only rarely occurs that life itself might be the point of life. When it stops, it stops.

Then what is life, if it is separated from goals, achievements and self? The answer is that it is a very frightening place indeed. While these hallucinations of comfort remain, while we sleep happily in velvet shackles it will grow more and more toxic teeth, its claws will seed themselves in the paw and the eyes will murder in their look. For what we are left with is a grey, leaden, acheing, menacing world of paranoia. Always the look must be cast sideways or back for fear. Is another taking one's place? Is one's wife faithful? Have I shut off the gas? Have I pension enough, food enough, time enough, will enough, enough, enough? Always the fear exists that after all my sternest efforts, weeping worries, brick upon brick of fortified building, mind hand-cuffs, bribed controls, prison bars, nothing remains, only perchance the whiff of a ghost moving through a wall with a smile, telling you that not a jot will be left to let the next occupier know that you ever were. So we will try even harder to make that mark of achievement, and in the trying that mark becomes harder to make.

What should we do with age? Sagging bellies and breasts, less sex? These must be hidden because they expose us to the one unmentionable; death. So we spend our short time in life, eating ridiculous foods, under the knife of the surgeon, some take lovers in the hope that they will convince them that they are not alone, and they are not ageing, that they are immortal. All these are gestures of hopelessness and fear.

How then might we train ourselves so that these foolish and irrational obsessions with the self and security may be laid to rest? The first must be to face without fear that which plagues our lives and demands our unrest, namely death. What does death demand, wherein lies such dread? The answer is of course, the eclipse of the soul, the loss of the preeminent I, the inexorable metamorphosis into nothing. We assume so much, pain, possible disaster, we see visions, we are always ahead of the game. Little realising that the instant of now is all we can occupy, we spend our time in a past that is ill- if not falsely-remembered or in a future that can never come. In a pitifully short life, we spend most of it not concentrating, missing our last very seconds. Let us then stop it.

Why are we so afraid of insecurity, of losing the esteemed I? Because we cannot visualise a world in which we have no control of all the things that properly matter, is perhaps an answer. We cannot accept the situation where our small, isolated, tinkling selves have no power. But this is the truth. Of all the things that matter most to us the beat of our heart and breath of our lungs must be the most important. If we try and hold our breath in order to conserve our most precious air, we die. We do not feel insecure in these matters for we know we have no choice. All we have power over is the feeble political now of our anthropocentric world.

Let us now assume that with the help of a Damascan bolt (probably from God) we can throw this desire for false security away. Such a bolt is often obligatory and often descends during a crisis. Our straining for security now gone, first we are aware of a certain elation and joy of the physically perceived freedom; then a great dullness as if a blind man was staring at a new world. A coldness now descends and covers us which is not unpleasant. The blindness is not one of the eyes, but of the soul, we live in this new earth of different forces and values, no longer can the self win or the will achieve, for here the terms are meaningless. Achieve what? Win? Also the outer skin becomes more malleable, stretchy. It now is in contact with and joins the outside space. The wall now fallen, we feel a similarity with things that were quite alien, we touch them as long-lost friends. We become them and they us. But still we feel sad, we feel the loss of an important person, we are bereaved. This is exactly what it is, for we have lost someone whom we loved more than it was possible to love anyone. We have lost ourselves. What a sense of emptiness, but also what strange far sounds we hear and what intoxicating thoughts we think. Now our new freedom makes us light, we wish to jump silently but slowly. Our new world begins (languidly) to assume a shape, is becoming focussed. Other colours, sounds, new smells start to force themselves on us. How could one have been so stupid, blind, deaf to something so obvious. Colour rushes to the cheeks of the long-insensitive. This is your real birth, but unlike the other neonate, you can now see, because you are not in the way. It all lies simply before you, no gauzes, no pillars, no blockings.

Warmth begins to return. Now we stand as explorers of this new world. New facts are ours, no one has seen this place before, this, our fast belief. What a sumptuous world it is, but not for long. We quickly realize with our tipsy soul that most of the people we talk to have not seen our truth and remain dumb and blind in a world we have forsaken. So we proselytize. We decide that armed with our amazing grace (the world sleeping soundly in its filthy sty), we will in almost Herculean vein sound réveillé with buckets of intuition and satori poking sticks at the ready.

In our joyful arrogance, we tend to choose the people we love *most*, dragging them unwilling and often screaming into a foreign world like so many refugees. We would deracinate them as we were so luckily and blissfully deracinated. We have assumed that because they are our favourites, their temperaments are like ours; no, *are* ours. So we are now all action and conversation, stunning the worldly world with our unworldly truth.

The die is cast, the globe now a spiritual wilderness (except my corner). All faiths are bigoted, all believers Satanic. Only one truth remains. If asked who was the bearer of this grail, the answer would be one of mystified hurt. We now begin to destroy people with our truth and power. Not one moment of rest can be found, none sacrosanct from the heavy guns. A talk of salad, shot to pieces, Jane Austen – anathema, Dickens – cretinous. Poetry happens to survive and most of art, but only when they light on a patch close to our ground. Music flies free, saying nothing controversial. Sometimes it's sentimental, but that is easily absorbed as meaningless in this orgiastic cauldron of self-righteousness. *What* righteousness? might be decently asked.

Thus the next stage begins. If you are lucky at this moment, a good friend of great wisdom will say, 'Why are you doing this? Don't you realise that all your so-called intuitions, your instants of satori, your blinding faith, your certitudes, are not necessarily truths but are merely facets of your own temperament?' Here is a megapoint. For in this remark the seeking for shareable standards jumps shrieking from its perch and our sight.

Is there nothing, then, that can be shared without feeble compromise and weak intellect? Is there nothing of which we can say we *know*, we *feel*, we *touch*, we *think* the same? The answer bellows, No.

Then what? Then an even newer world, even more lonely, a country in which not even a colour can be relied upon to bring fellowship. In this cleaner world any propaganda whatever, whether it be of word, picture or sound becomes useless. All stored knowledge wilful conversion of the less strong and malleable. If every soul is born unique and full of possibilities, it makes absolute sense that every idea absorbed which is not of the new soul is in fact a mark of some other soul which in this solipsistic world can only influence whether in the terms of corruption or benediction. All this collected accoutrement can only be the blubbering of various egoists who were also seeking for the truth.

The outcome is a further insidious warmth, and from now on we will say very little. We have now occupied this solitary world in two ways, the first with surprise and memories of the old life, the second with this straight warm acceptance. The self-scales now fall fast, plummet from our eyes. Now and only now can actionless love begin. The question of good is at first only seen afar off out of the corner of the eye, then becomes insistent, banging for entrance hammer in hand, becomes pre-eminent. If all is lonely, useless, flawed and terminal, why do I wish for love and good? Because I feel it is there. The final stage commences.

Here a dilemma faces us that has faced spiritual philosophers since the organisation of thought. What

can one say, when words are redundant? The area we
now occupy is one of feeling and belief. The loneliness
we have considered previously leaves off, falls quite
away as an echo of the protected self of a former life.
Having perceived, felt and admitted good we can in
its ethereal train see benediction, grace and spiritual
justice. We see these not from a far off nest, but from
their souls. Evil now becomes only a waste of time and
a possession of the old dead self. Good is now only for
good. Rewards can't be had for the receiver is in fact
the giver. Serious joy occupies time, a thing which in
itself now has ceased to have measure, being above selfish number. This joy has a physical effect. Each step
will be remarkable and will foot aside reason. Tears will
flood unsuspecting moments. Good action will spring
unbidden into place. People around are amazed and
glad. Life for those close to you becomes easier, the
tensions of the self-struggle over. Work, once an area
of achievement and winning, becomes a game. Fun is
the game. Of course, technical matters still predomi-
nate, but they are ingrained and of second nature and
become incorporated into a blessed carelessness which
removes detonators and leaves the doer the space
in which to singularly be. When the new active is
observed in the task, people will be amazed at the joy
being carelessly chucked about. They will wish to be
part of the sport. So joys beget joys and love, love.

Love plays a higher and higher role. What once
seemed an arid intellectual idea, the unity of all things,

is now an absolute fact. This thought grasped-at so hopefully and never touched has become commonplace. The power of the begetter springs from the same source as that of the begotten. With the ineffable, ubiquitous God, all things created, part-created or about to be are one. We are now the power of life. We are in it, alongside it, above it, below it, we are the force of life. We are God.

This consolation is almost a deceit. Can you imagine a better deal? The gift of a worn, fearful, dying paranoic shell swapped for careless Eternity?

10

I feel that I should be bombarding you with winsome and riotously funny anecdotes, the ones you can never remember when asked by a radio or television journalist. I promise that I will not disappoint, because I will dredge some up from the sludge at the bottom of my mind. But before this happens I must insist that all these psycho-philosophic burblings are inextricably bound to the Voice, to the way music is seen, accepted, categorised, performed. There can be no separating the inner from the outer man, therefore if you want the funny bits you've got to work for them.

Now perhaps you begin to see a dilemma. I have

caused this by too much thought. But this old process is such a seducer, gives so much pleasure, so much pain. It was once said to me by John Shirley Quirk that he thought that singing was no job for a thinking man, and a cow-bell rang in my mind. It is, of course, vitally important to think when singing. First the role must be analysed. Can Don Ottavio in *Don Giovanni* be made to look like a character viable for the stage or is he doggedly going to remain in his wimpish guise? If he can serve a dramatic function, then life must be injected into him. How shall we do this? Then we must think into the nature of his two arias. Is *dalla sua pace* simply a declaration of vapid love, or could it, if sung in a more rock-like solid block way be heard as the declaration of controlled, strong passion? This is the kind of thinking which is called into play. It is concerned, as you can see, mostly with the psycho-logical assessment of character and dramatic analysis of motive. It is concerned with spacing of phrases in the vocal mind. It is interested in logistics of move-ment. The real moments of recreation occur in the instant and flow sometimes but not always from the kind of thought that I describe. The feeling remains strong that only a small department of the mind has been exercised by these disciplines. A great, no, *vast* area of the mind remains dark and unused. It is as if you lived in a huge house but only occupied the front rooms downstairs. All the rest of the house is left dark, shuttered and forgotten, for all practical intents not existing. But a worrying itch is present or perhaps it is a knocking as if something is trying to be heard, trying to get out. You then ask yourself whether you have the courage to look for the sound, to nail the itch. Will you find death, chaos? Now the part of the mind not used in singing comes into play, is recognised and is released. The essentially non-pragmatic part of the brain is now working and leads you into those areas of concept like God, Love, Goodness. It leads into your soul. It asks uncomfortable questions and receives answers commensurate. Suddenly all the forgotten rooms, the boarded-up cupboards, are shining with light as if a switch has been thrown. We see these chambers lit for the first time, radiant in amethyst; then red and green stars appear and after a time a phosphorescent brightness that we have not seen before. The contents of the rooms are revealed in all their possibilities and instantly the sense of something missing is gone. I repeat that this sensation is indeed a heady seducer. The hidden self can now burrow like Keats' mole, endlessly searching, sometimes finding but delighting in the chase. What a relief for the strutting man of the boards, publicly always at account, personally, at a slip, in danger of penury.

11

My last obsession is now engaged and you won't
have to wait much longer for the stories. 'Look at you
now, what a messy eater. It's all down your tie; yes,
you have spilt your coffee, yes! There is marmalade on
your shirt. I don't remember offering you marmalade.
It hadn't set, that's why it's running over you. Go
upstairs, get washed, have a shave, do anything you
like but get back here in time for the stories.' Thank
God he's gone. I'll be quick, I promise.

I've always believed that we are not actively desired
by our parents but are begot for two reasons. The first
of these is the ought of Nature, Erda, to fill her soul and
occupy her vacuum. The second appears when the
besotted lovers in their judders convince themselves
that the fruit of their true passion will even in some
small way represent their most perfect godlike selves.
They also, perhaps without being conscious, feel that
in the seed lives their only chance of immortality.

This created seed in time assumes his standing and
begins to disagree. He is offended, he came totally

unbidden into this vale and was not privy to their ecstatic nonsense or their hackneyed plans. Love made manifest now must live for seventy years and they are lost for him as they are for themselves. However the plans generally concern, depending on class, making sure that he will have a better life than they had, or they will make sure that the comfort of their lives is continued in him by 'willing' him their 'goodies'. (By the way, this second type won't know him at all, having sent him away to school at five years and before this having entrusted him into the care of a trained nanny.) Their garnered harvests over the previous centuries have ensured that they do not have to think, and they will guarantee this for him. So their trusts ring like a cracked bell before evensong and the anthem is the second of S. Wealth's seven settings, 'Those whom the Gods wish to destroy, they first make rich' in A major. In Bethesda in Wales, in a square God box with balconies, the other famous hymn of I. M. Proove, 'Grasping souls dissuade in a blink' is being sung lustily.

The seed, who is now me, is thrown into an education system (if the plan has worked) which I consider at best incompetent and at worst cynical. If we really wished the best for our young ingress we would respect the fact that he comes to us new. This is not to say that he does not haul about the millions of years of others bestowed on him by careless nature. But nevertheless he appears – I mean, I appear in the world without notable prejudice. The education I am then given consists in all cases of the personal visions of geniuses and madmen. I don't remember being taught in school any of the important things: being taught of death, of the passionate personal love I could feel for God, of Trahearne's vision of corn, of the non-didactic ineffable soul of Mozart, of the love of Van Gogh. However I was taught many things, most of them perfect instruments to fix me into the faded sayings of the seers and the actions of the self-protected assembly. Morality was a force not of good but of pragmatism (of keeping society together), art a remembered assembly of various misunderstood truisms. I must only succeed through others' words and eyes. Poetry I learned was something for the sensitive, usually more concerned with the dandruff on collars than the life or death search for God. I was prey to the propaganda of the bereft thinking of man's idle and frightened heart. This is on the plus side.

The cynical is that the education especially of the two most constant fountains, Oxford and Cambridge, is geared to ensure that the government of the country remains petrified but stable. When a senior parrot of the civil service falls silently from his perch, another will be ready, shiny-beaked, with the colours of all the rainbow in his tail. Let us therefore be immortal by sentiment and accept the concept by collaboration. I know that this theory of the conspiracy of education seems paranoid but I announce it nevertheless, as I find it hard to ignore the evidence before me.

And yet there rests in my anarchic soul the desire to belong to things of little worth. Hence the need to be accepted by gentlemen's clubs and hence the need to accept the honours of the state. Commander Tear does not wish to speak of these peccadillos as a son of the working class man working his way into the higher strata or as a fifth columnist worm eating away silently into the fabric of Society. He would say however that it flatters his ego pleasantly but not unduly. I do believe with Conrad that the one who joins is lost. I will join only that which brings me closer to God, to whom I will not bring masses of impedimenta, but only naked love. Meanwhile I will not push too hard on the big chariot and will not get covered too heavily in dust (with luck).

12

What has this to do with singing? I suppose very little except perhaps to illustrate the paucity for this kind of thought offered in notes. However, this slippery exercise was never intended to be about singing but about one singular singer's view of his job and his context in the world and his reaction to it.

'You haven't quite got all the marmalade off your tie and look! you're dropping toast out of your sleeves, but I think you look a bit cleaner. Your timing is quite good, however. Go on, sit down.'

'No thanks, I'll stand.'

I now paint a Rubenesque scene. I am looking at one (later it must be admitted), namely the Adoration of the Magi. It is evensong, 5.30 on the dot, a November evening. I am standing in the front stalls – the boys' stalls – in the greatest example of English perpendicular architecture. This is the chapel of King's College, Cambridge. The fan vaulting is dancing, about to take off in a stony *la volta*. The light, a mixture of late day and snuffling candles, defies the eyes. (This was the light you could smell. I can smell it now.) An assembled group of various worshippers, choir afficionados, groupies and pederasts stand transfixed within their worlds in this petrified womb of time. The Flemish windows catch the rays of the last of cold day and Abraham scowls, hating Isaac in his thoughts. The yellows, the blues keep their distance, the greens are not jealous.

'Are you all concentration? Is your mind's eye sufficiently keen to take this in?' 'I'm really trying now.' Those Gibbons woods would be paradise to his namesakes. Now see the soft light of the wittering candles against the hood of the don who walks, spider-like affected, to read the lesson. 'Thanks be to God' echoes through the building, going flat as it recedes. The organ begins its antiphon, the moment of sanctity nears. You must know that moment well, the one you remember, when everybody looks as if he has eaten the canary but knows no one can see the feathers.

The choir walks noiselessly in, dressed in passionate red. What clean-shaven young men! What an example! Each and every a seed realised, if not in total purity, at least in serenity.

It happens to be men only day, a Wednesday, that's why we are standing in the front stalls. Millars (the pub) opens at six (we will certainly have to get a shift on with the psalms) to dispense to the young and innocent a brew, a truly godlike drop, called Worthington's. This has long since passed, its present taste a penumbra of its character and potency in those far-off days. But I digress.

We assume our places, open our books, scrape our throats quite silently for any vestige of mucus likely to sully the note. The leader gives us two beats for nothing with two fingers (I must add held consciously tight together) and the act of worship in song constitutes itself again, instant echoes of old, long-gone notes, deposited in the stone crannies waiting patiently to be released day by day by their contemporary children. Unknown to us and unknown to the congregation or audience as we thought them, the lead alto and a fine chap has a vicious cold. (This condition is common in the treacherous fens.) We are singing the Lamentations of Jeremiah, Tallis at his tensest. Aleph forms itself from the strands of sound. Then an outburst. Ah! Aaa! Aaaar! Aluemph!! the alto has sneezed. In his panic not to send the nasal detritus down his cassock he has wrenched a handkerchief from the right-hand pocket of his pants. Before I tell you the outcome of this action (let him remain frozen in mid-wrench), I must tell you that this man was unduly fond of ladies, not to say a womaniser. I can say that no man in Cambridge could sleep peacefully in his bed for fear of daughters or wife when the choir was up.

The outcome of the snatch is a miracle. Showers of gold look to their laurels. Sightings of the virgin are drab, even those of her the size of a bottle of wine are commonplace, for out of the pocket and across the chancel are thrown – no, I think I mean strewn – a hail of prophylactics, or johnnies as we call them. Watch the uproar. The drapes and shafts of Bernini have known no equal. Surplices fly like nimbus clouds, putti weep. Tallis blushes and the congregation hides behind its flawless face.

13

'Oh, I see you're more interested now. I tell you what, go and get yourself a book of Milton and hold it in your hand. Then open it to *Paradise Lost*, it will do you good.' 'Not finished yet.' 'Look up the bits about wings. They're everywhere.'

This next story is really a rough and nasty one. I was on one of those tedious trips across the Atlantic. I wasn't just going to the eastern side but to Los Angeles, twelve hours' flying from Heathrow. The flight proceeded quite normally for an hour or two, hot and cold running nurses, 'I'm Ugly, your hostess,' and tracks of me on the inflight earphones. This was the time when British Airways tended to play Ben Luxon and my Victorian ballads *ad nauseam*. The attempt to drink, in alcohol, my extra fare had long petered-out, my neighbour had 'upchucked' decorously a few times and the film was of such boredom that I chose to watch the clouds. Then I noticed it for the first time. It was the same old 'it' of course, the one which I've explained to you earlier. The pin-pricks hot and cold were definitely setting themselves up. I for a moment questioned whether these symptoms were physical or mental and found them decidedly the first. 'Oh, Christ,' I murmured, not hoping for much help. My projection of the performing fear to come, stopped me from eating, sleeping, drinking or reading for the rest of the journey. The plane put down. I rushed for the door, a sardine like the rest, passed through the hideously inimical customs. 'Got any pecans?' and not carrying any baggage, this is my way, proceeded to the warm, fresh kerosened air.

It is my wont to travel with one small Maremeko bag. In it lie all the necessities for at least five weeks of sojourn. I pack the washing things and lie them in the right-hand corner, pressed firmly down. Then with much care – no, obsessional caring – I roll first my trousers (the braces always play up), making sure there are no original creases. Around these are placed socks and knickers in necessary numbers. A foundation is thus achieved. Now comes the tail coat, that anarchist of packing. With much thought and dexterity each rebelling tail is caught and subdued, and each watered-silk lapel contained. Now I think it's done. But this is far from the truth. The shirt or shirts (I always think that I can make one last three concerts with luck. This luck is often helped by changing after the event, so that tomato ketchup or mango chutney does not transform the white cloth into memories of Ypres or Calcutta) is or are then packed plus tie, a strangely amorphous and flighty object, many times sporting the blood of quick and ill-judged shaves. Then come the day shirts, usually darkly hued and instantly washable, socks and not forgotten but niftily inserted into the washbag, blacking for the one pair of shoes that must to through wind, mire, snow, salt, sand, stones, shit, rain, dead pigeons, whatever. Finally I pack my books. If I am going to America (as I was on this occasion) I take few, as I know that this is the pulsating heart of published literature, especially that in which I am interested. If not America, then I pack many. Finally I put in the score of the piece I shall be performing.

I was met by a nice girl putting in overtime without

pay for the Symphony. This job, meeting the faces on the puffs (I use this noun in strict eighteenth-century way) must in some ways be glamorous, but I bet it wears off pretty quickly. She took me in her car downtown. This word has meant, and I think always will mean to me, drabness, ugliness, prostitution, aggression, hopelessness. It seems to mean to them excitement, liveliness, sex, quick air, where it's at. I was deposited at my hotel, walked with small-pocked card-key in hand to my room, opened the door. Was it a football pitch or a field of synthetic corn? Whichever, I hung up my gear and struggled Gulliver-like through the fibres until with relief I found a bed the size of Spain on which I readily and happily collapsed and slept.

I have forgotten to tell you that I was engaged to sing *Messiah* conducted by Sir Neville Marriner (or 'Nev' as he then was). The soprano was Sheila Armstrong, the others wisps of forgotten *Messiahs*. It was to be in Hollywood. The inexorable itch progressed, mightily encouraged by the new air and the meetings with long-lost brothers eager to discuss viral political trends. The dark tunnel descended, the paranoia placed first one and then the other foot on my feeble shoulders.

The morning and my awakening came quite normally with dull awareness, but for a second. Panic of remembrance and burning throat then brought on the Niagara Sweats. The world turned on its dark side. A morning rehearsal had been called and I went to it as if to an execution. I haven't mentioned that this concert was to take place at a venue beloved by the glitterati; pop stars gyrate there, Percy Grainger was married there. It sits in a bowl (natural, I believe) in the Hollywood hills and has its name, Hollywood Bowl, carved and whitewashed into the hapless rock above lest it should forget where and what it is. The place would hold at a pinch about 20,000 souls and certainly with 17,000 there would be room enough for knitting.

At the rehearsal I teetered along my vocal lines rather like a trapeze artist in heavy boots. Then I was invited to lunch by the management. I thought it would never end. Feeling sicker by the instant I could not eat or even taste, I could not concentrate on the almost Shakespearian recitation of the fares of the day by a hatchet-faced waitress with all the charm of world war three. I went to bed and woke up hoarse, with a hard-raw-steak *haché* feeling just under the chords, about to attack.

In a stadium of this size microphones are deemed a necessary adornment to the singer for the aural gratification of the multitude. I would say that singers are most suspicious of anything resembling a microphone, firstly hating the control it gives someone else over the sound you produce, secondly because with it comes the mute criticism that your voice is too small ('Oh, yes, she has a voice like a pearl,' very white with a hole in the middle) and thirdly because you might be being surreptitiously recorded with no extra money. Anyway, the night, as it has the unpleasant way of doing, finally arrived. I knew that I was in severe trouble. If, however, the rising infection would stay put for another two and a half hours, I might survive. Sometimes with concerts, there are literally minutes, crucial minutes, between the possibility or impossibility of work. It was a typical Los Angeles evening, humid, an odd arrangement of air, with the sweet-smelling flowers and the heady scent of pine-trees mixed with benzine. The music started and I became resigned and unnaturally calm. I said to myself, 'Come on, this is only *Messiah*, you've sung it over two hundred times, it's not *Siegfried*, you've got a mike, throw your fear to God.' The fearful outcome was that at mid-*Messiah* God affected to drop the catch. *Comfort ye* and *Every valley*, the tenor opening had been tentative, to put it mildly. With this hideous burning sensation in the larynx and enough gunge to sink a battleship lurking, I had manipulated the voice like a skilled driver on a mountain precipice, moving at first around the catarrh, then under it, above it and to the side. With the arrival of the Easter music, *Thy rebuke hath broken his heart* etc., I began to take on the mantle of Frank Sinatra. There is an hour between the tenor's first utterance and this section. The state of voice had worsened considerably in the meantime, the first song having inflamed the already-sick chords. Anyhow, I moved even closer to the microphone. I was tempted like the famous crooner to sing *I left my voice in mid-Atlantic, high in the sky* . . . etc. I just made this section. *But thou didst not leave his soul in Hell,* I hoped that this would be a good omen.

Now, the time between this number and the final *He that dwelleth in Heaven* and *Thou shalt break them* is perhaps twenty-five minutes. These proved crucial. For as I in panic tested my voice quickly, aside, 'Bee - Bee, Mee - Mee, Fee - Fee' (this last with a prayer), like a demented road-runner, I found that it diminished until my efforts were rewarded with only silence and sweating. I leaned to Sheila and whispered, 'Do you think you can manage *Thou shalt break them*?

She, to her eternal glory, courage and professional-ism, nodded in the affirmative and I with steady re-lieved tread and followed by 34,000 eyes walked out, pausing only to see the colours of grey, yellow and white chameleoning Neville's face. Strolling lightly (the pressure now gone) down from the Bowl among the increasingly powerful scents now released by the cooling night air, I heard my aria being sung quite exquisitely with every run placed and articulated. The audience were hearing a world premiere of that aria. How many knew, I wondered. Some idiot in the morn-ing press asserted that the soprano did not seem quite at ease in her last aria, but what can you expect from journalists (more of this troupe later)? One question remained. Would I get paid? To the manager's credit the answer was Yes.

48

14

'How did you like that one, then?'

I look up and find my colleague mightily translated. I have always loved Milton but never so estimated the power of his word, for there before me hanging upside-down on a box (the bigger sort) of Swan Vestas matches is a bat of the Pipistrelle variety. He turns his sweet head over his right shoulder, licks his teeth with his tongue and squeaks in his lowest tone especially for my benefit: 'Very much indeed, thank you.'

As I now have the unique chance of not only communication, but conversation with an animal I become excited and say: 'Would you be unduly disturbed if I asked you a question or three?'

'No,' was chirruped in my direction.

'In that case,' (assuming an indulgent tone), 'tell me what you think of the voice-production of the human. What does it convey? Is it beautiful? Can it disturb the trees? Can it make your earth shake as it can ours? Is it the ultimate, with its running words, its communication?'

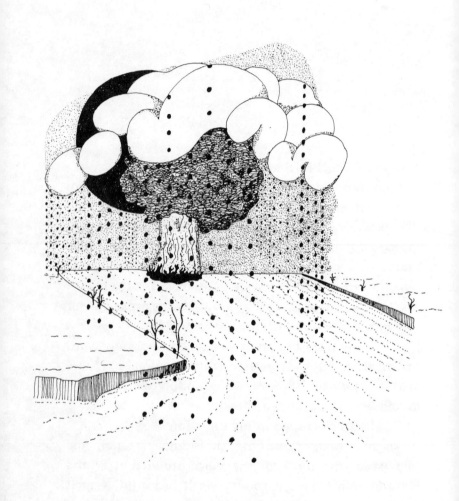

'That's six questions in one,' he said, 'but you'll only get one answer.'

'And what is that?' I spoke as high as I could and in his accent, a sort of Dutch one with Glaswegian highlights, in order to make him feel comfortable.

'You see, there never has been a worthwhile communication between us creatures and you masters. Saint Francis had a good try but even he saw us with a patronising eye. I hope that I'm not being unduly difficult but it really has been an insurmountable task for us. You ask me, an impotent bat, to comment on your voice-production, knowing all the while that whatever I say will be interpreted according to your own rules. If I say that your voice range is fearfully weak and that your carrying power is pathetic, you will become angry and say, well what does it matter, you're only a bat. I promise you, and as part of it I think I'm qualified to speak, that your anthropomorphism has destroyed the unity of God's world. You believe that all blackbirds, green birds, pink, blue, red breasts, corncrakes, bitterns, nuthatches, flamingoes, nightingales, all birds sing to mark their territory, but I tell you that they sing for more fun than you could ever know. They are not separate from God, they sing and when they sing all of creation sings. They don't watch their songs. You think your conquest of the air a miracle. We did it when God was the membrane of a bee. How can we live in collaboration when you only accept your rules? I can dive into a cleft without breaking a nail, catch bugs on the wing with my radar, make love, sing, communicate in a highly-educated way, can loop the loop for pure joy, no need for money, no question of applause. Can you name one of your lot who lived simply for living without making damn stupid didactic points or need the paying for them? Come on, answer me now and come clean. How can I compare in beauty if you have decided that your look is the mean? I have to you an unattractive appearance. I am black, like a hairy cockroach. I seem to have the most unappealing arms, simply because my hands are bigger than yours; my nose, it is true, is a scrunched one rather like a bell-push. But I can assure you that we find ourselves remarkably attractive. As for our singing, we can so far outshoot you that you are baffled by deafness in the heights of our colloratura. And one more thing, when we are in the thrall of being no more, we don't whimper, cry, bewail and attempt to ensure our wonderful selves an eternity of a similar mediocrity to that we have lived when alive. We simply fall to the floor and are consumed by the habitually needy. Death is so important to you two-standers. You seem to regard it as an enemy. It waits for you in forest, meadow, desert, in light, dusk or dark. It seems always to strike where it is least wanted. Dearest baldy, *it* doesn't strike, it can't, because you are death at every moment, you carry it in your heart. You bear it in your soul, yet you will not welcome it or even admit it to your hearth full of nature's best fruit and surrounded by golden corn with heads about to explode and cover your whole lives with love and good. The beer fountains forth but you will not drink, the wine begs your lips but you turn your heads. What you have not realised is that the man with the long scythe has always occupied your homes, has always lived with you. But once you have accepted this and some of you have, then the scales leap from your lids and the battle coins are lifted from your eyes, and that life once only treasured because of its imminent end, assumes a different proportion and dimension and colour and is seen as itself, a blessing once accepted that will gimlet love around and give you glimpses of the eye that cannot see itself but rests within.'

Exhausted by such an effusion of love, my little friend fell dead from the box and looked like a tiny black broken umbrella.

Slightly embarrassed by the power of his answer and also feeling more than a little apologetic on behalf of the 'two-standers', I had been about to ask him (to lighten the air a little) whether or not he would like me to tell him a short and terse anecdote. Sadly, he cannot answer me now, but I will nevertheless tell it as a kind of 'In Memoriam Bat'.

15

Years ago, when bats had the membranes of bees and God in his inscrutable way watched and ruled us in short trousers, I used to sing with a remarkable singer, namely Alfred Deller. In those days early music was performed from the inside. It took its spring from the passion of the words and lines and was not too concerned with imposed style. Fashions have changed so dramatically that authenticity (the concept cannot exist as the only authentic performance must be the first) has become a matter of high chic founded on ill-understood vocal theses of the seventeenth century and implemented almost only by the strings with an imposition of no vibrato as sound and continuous bulges in the place of onward-moving living line. The rest of the orchestra, wind, drums, etc. remains virtually indistinguishable from the modern band playing out of tune.

Alfred Deller, as most people know, was the man who single-handedly revived the lost art of counter-tenor or alto singing. Once popular in the early seventeenth century in England, Purcell himself being a notable exponent, it fell into disuse and its place was taken by the foreign import of the castrato. Farinelli, as mentioned earlier, was the most famous. Alfred's sound was extremely beautiful but unusual, and the less than mentally robust were often quite bemused by it. Just to remind you, it is an unearthly disembodied sound produced by bringing only a certain part of the larynx into play. It has also sometimes been known in the less salubrious of choir dives as the 'cock-alto'. Deller was one of the great communicators of our time. He had a perfect sense of where the important moment lay and would direct these bars like minute arrows straight to the heart of the listener. I remember that I was once moved to tears by his singing of Thomas Campion's *Never weather-beaten sail, more willing bent to shore.*

Back to the tale. We were singing in Leverkusen, not one of Germany's most beautiful cities, and were invited to drinks and sandwiches after the concert. (In those days – and these, come to think of it – one had to be remarkably fleet-footed to beat the committee and public to the food. As the gannets descended there was precious little for the artists and we had the handicap of changing, too.) During this particularly glorious repast a woman of uncertain age came up to Deller and with a strong, thick German accent, said in English: 'You are eunuch, Herr Deller?'

He paused, considered most theatrically and then from his considerable height, replied: 'I'm sure you mean unique, Madam.'

55

16

Sitting quite happily that same night in my room watching tele with a quarter of an eye, trying to use it as a German tutor, I decided to abandon the whole affair and go to bed. I therefore undressed, and having seen a Gideon bible, I sat totally naked and decided to read a few chapters of Job before sleeping. I was aroused out of my comatose but receiving state by a very smart blow on my right shoulder. I turned and saw a small man in eighteenth-century gear. The white-powdered wig sat beautifully, fitting a neat head with definite Mediterranean features. The clothes would have become a senior bullfighter on his night off. He wore very high-heeled shoes with gold buckles, silver (almost lamé) tights, deep aubergine velvet breeches and orange waistcoat with Chinese designs in gold, the most effulgent of lace shirts, and all this covered by a coat of velvet black. You might say I was surprised. But my surprise was octuple when he said in the most gross English, liberally seeded with German colloquialisms: 'Well, arschloch,' (arse-hole), 'explain your shit.'

'What do you mean?' I retorted.

'You f.....g well know what,' he observed.

With meek servilitude (because I felt that this whole situation could become difficult) and (I thought) with great subtlety, I said, in language to fit his clothes: 'Sir, I believe you have the advantage of me.'

'You bet the crap I have,' he said, directly.

'Then tell me of your slight,' I rejoindered, also directly.

'Listen, turd, I didn't spend the odd half-hour working for piles like you to ruin the output.'

Quite clearly the little man was overwrought so I decided with politeness to humour him.

'My name is Bob Tear: now sit down and tell me yours.'

'You sit on the crapper and then I'll tell you mine.'

It transpired that he was Wolfie Moiezert of some fame in earlier times. It took my stupid brain only a few seconds more to unravel the accent and realise that I was in the very near vicinity of God.

'I've listened to you, scheiss-kopf' (shit-head) 'ruin Idomeneo, Arbaces, the high priest, Tamino, Monostratos, the armed man, Don Ottavio, Pedrillo, Basilio, Belmonte, my fortieth *and* Jupiter symphonies, my C minor Mass, my (or rather, Franz Xavier's) Requiem, in fact a fair arse-wipe of my work. Why did, rather, do you do this?'

I answered, hesitatingly and open, 'I tried to understand but can only with *my* mind and preconception and soul. All those heinous crimes I committed against you were committed in *your* honour. But how can you, a composer, however great, hope to control your work? I can well see that Rembrandt or Velasquez or Turner or Lear gave up the ghost when the work was over. They could understand that once on the wall, the picture was up for all means of individual misinterpretation, but at least they had drawn what they knew. With you, Wolfy, you rely on people like me. Did you ever dream that I would "interpret" your dots? Did you ever get a show half-near to perfect?'

'When I write my Symphonies, you know the ones I toss away between the red and the black, then I hear perfect music. I always heard Constanze perfectly sung as I was writing it. So I didn't need your kind and certainly don't now. I can't tell you what these so-called original instrument versions do to my work. If the perpetrators knew that I spent all my working life trying to stop people playing like this, and to make them spiel an oily singing line they'd die. However, there was a catch. I needed money so people had to perform my pieces, and from that moment they became imperfect. I never heard a perfect *Entführung*, the tenors always had imaginary colds, they wouldn't even drink cold beer, but would heat it with a hot iron prong, the women seemed always to have had the curse. No, it was rough, I can tell you. And then up would come an "intelligent" singer and start to theorise about my dots and analyse the characters and before I knew where I was the piece was mine no more. I could hear shadows of it behind the posturing ego, but only shadows.'

'How can I let you through, Bruce?' (He liked being called Bruce.) 'How can I stop getting in the way?'

Bruce answered.

'How long is eternity?'

I had no idea and began to march down the labyrinthine ways of my mind filled with ill-digested facts sloughed off like snake skins. But I was forced to admit my ignorance.

'Well, how long is eternity, Amadeo?'

'Just time for a laugh,' he answered and confirmed. 'If you treat my music with this holiness, with the sadness implicit in the smile, and the shortness implied and the innocence of a true reaction (not one complicated by analysis) then my music will speak.'

I had heard his aphorism before but was too polite to say. I began to sense his person fading; his clothes and stockings grew hazy, it was as if a theatrical gauze was being thrown around him. Quickly I asked him a final question.

'Tell me, Maestro, why do you use such filthy language?'

With a voice sounding from way off, he said: 'I tend to wish not to disappoint my fans of the twentieth century, and when I meet one I always curse and speak in this foetid way. After all, if I didn't they might think Peter Shaffer wasn't speaking the truth, and I wouldn't want that, now, would I?'

With that he disappeared and I haven't seen him again, at least, not up to now.

17

It really must be so difficult for composers. They put in marks and dynamics and tempo markings to guide us, but these are worse than useless, weak signposts in a wild and dangerous landscape. Some composers are so conscious of this weakness of control that they virtually lose interest in the piece. Benjamin Britten was one of these. Once an opera was cast and performed, that for him (as he had cast it) was the definitive version and any future workings with different people could only result in the deterioration of the piece. For us, however, rubbing shoulders with genius and working – no, creating – with it, is supremely satisfying. More of B. Britten later.

I should like now to discuss very generally the weeping question of authentic music. We all know that the only authentic performance is the first. It is the unique one and cannot be repeated. We know that period instruments are modern period instruments. We know that seventeenth-century treatises are quite likely to have been misinterpreted. So let us put all this aside as dubious in the extreme and let us see what we are left with. What we hear is a new, perfectly unique way of playing old music. It is chic, it is opinionated, it is radical, instantly recognisable. It might be interesting to ask why such a new form of music should have happened when it did, and why it was spawned in England. (I insist that the authentic music movement is an essentially English phenomenon.)

In a newspaper article not so long ago Nicholas Maw the composer speculated that this new old music had flourished directly because of the paucity of understandable modern music. There is perhaps some truth in this. But I believe that the answer more readily lies in the nature of the English who formed and sold the style. There is deeply rooted in the soul of the middle-class English man a deep hatred of vulgarity and an equally deep mistrust of that which is not under the direct control of the intellect, which is emotion. Emotions are perhaps interesting but fundamentally vulgar. They are interesting to analyse, but awkward to cope with when they very occasionally break through the shell of imposed control. Raw emotional commitment tends to lead to excess which in its turn tends to lead to success. Success can only last if it is treated in a professional way. This small band of bourgeois English therefore tend to find both professionalism and success, vulgar. Gardens with only white flowers, dresses in pastel colours, simple shoes, no one is rich, affairs are conducted with understanding, everyone is blameless. With this attitude it is reasonable that they should prefer the good try, prefer amateur sport, amateur shots at painting, amateur cooking, amateur music.

New-old music is a direct outcome of this tempera-ment. The lack of passionate line, the out-of-tuneness, the Toc-H commitment all suit perfectly. This new style is a last resurgence of Bloomsbury, of gentility, of vicious docility, the older visual stigmata of haversack and sandal being replaced by the aural ones of bloodless fainting line and anorexic soul.

18

Having got this far, and I must admit it's not very far in ink spilt and I use the verb with true caution, what is appearing and happening – or should these two be reversed? – is not an autobiography but a dainty noveletta of the soul. Perhaps the two are the same. Anyway, I scan these long-hand, short lines in the vain hope of finding a thread. This defeats me but does leave me inquiring into the need for such. Is there such a thing? In living, especially in our viewing of the past, we tend to see our occupancy of the time as a sinuous, logical line with a few unexplained and unexpected blips and blotches let it be said, but never-theless as something that makes logical but mad sense, a predestined plan perhaps, being read as it should; a heavenly walk downhill to the sea past trees, bears, snakes, keys, houses, cups, lakes and walls. I believe we construct this plan to give ourselves a feeling of belonging, to force ourselves to believe that there is a plan for us. We will never be comforted by the obvious truth, this being: we are born and then we die. There is no continuity of action in life apart from second slipping inexorably into a different unconnected second, and this itself is an anthropocentric construction. All things happen when and as they do. All nature is as the Japanese say TSU-JAN, roughly translated, 'Of itself so'. Alan Watts says, 'Life is something that keeps happening.' I think that we should not make dubious threads of the separate gifts of God; they tend to make us miss the moment. This thread is the reason why the novel is an inimical form to me. Now with no bridge passage, no link, no thread I will take you to a fantasy.

19

I am sitting in a green meadow. What other colour, you might say, if you were listening, but I insist on using the obvious adjective because it was of a different green, it was translucent as if the meadow was lit from below. In this meadow are millions of flowers all

of a perfect height and all carry their colours forward in a strange way. I almost took cover from the shells of red, blue, puce, yellow that threatened my body. This idyllic field sloped southward and at the bottom was flowing a large stream, almost a river, at the right pace. It was silver and gnarled brown in patches like a birch. Above me, hidden by the sun, a skylark now mocked a tired man. I sleep and see a vision in my dream. It begins as an ancient echo and gradually grows warmer until I am aware that something very, very, very important is about to happen. I now know what it is. I am formulating the secret of eternal happiness for all men. Within seconds my idea has been made manifest in the form of a word. 'In the beginning was the word.' Could this be the word of the end? The word is (I won't keep it from you)

SERPHOWGLUMITY.

(The fourth and fifth letters may be pronounced separately or together.)

Even in my unconscious, the knowledge that I have out-lucked them all spreads a deep and happy heaviness on my body. My nose (pointed heavenwards in mute respect) begins to accept the gifts of this, it must be an Elysian field, and breathes in minute grasses, pollens, seeds and all kinds of jetsam and the bits of dead nature and begins in its torpid state to reject them. But instead of sneezing them out explosively, it tolerates them, then accepts and finally snores. The mute proboscis is now an alp-horn. But to my dreaming soul, the notes are not of music, but of tanks and battle and of quite different theatres. Every juddered breath small-arms fire, every ronfle, rounds of bitter Kalashnikovs.

Could my word have caused this affray? I know that this is no affray but a war, a world war, a seventh world war. How could my super-word have such power, such charge?

The answer is that the brilliant intellect of man had unravelled it in quick time and discovered that this word of genius was an amalgam of the words: GLORY, POWER, RIGHTS, and HUMILITY. What could be better for man's need of a message and need of self-righteousness than all these super-concepts unified and perhaps soon to be satisfied? No, let me not be modest; deified. Unfortunately, many various scholars had thought differently about the order of the words. Those who need something desperately in order to gainsay their unacceptable self had nippily joined in and formed factions. The factions soon became schisms. Everyone joined in. Soon the world was aflame with hate. Bullets whizzed and people in millions died for 'anities' and 'isms'. But just as the slaughter became unbearable for the future of mankind, I roused myself in my dream and shouted – bellowed – through a yellow hailer with red piping.

'STAND UP SERPHOWGLUMITY'

The guns were stilled, the cries only of the dying left in the warm grassy-milk air.

'STAND UP SERPHOWGLUMITY'

No one answered. No one stood. Everyone went home for tea (at least those who were not already dead) for they knew no one called Serphowglumity. They would wait there until they could, for fear of death, commit themselves to another concept. Perhaps they would die for a flag, who knows?

I woke up and decided to stay where I was, for it was still fair in the sky.

20

I have always had a difficult time evaluating the need of criticism. Critics are generally extremely nice people, well-educated, and good dinner guests. This being so the fact that they have chosen their profession – or perhaps it could have chosen them? – fills me with unease. No, that is over-stated. I mean that the idea that a life can be given to this profession makes me doubt them. Liking them, I find this unsettling. I know that you are all expecting me now to summon-up an imaginary character. Would he be dressed in a green corduroy jacket with leather or leatherette elbow patches? Could he be wearing grey flannel trousers and loafer shoes? Might he be balding authoritatively and carrying a pair of fifties specs with heavy anthracite frames on his nose? He could, I suppose, also be walking with a slight stoop and carrying a rolled, no, a folded newspaper under his right arm.

Well, I'm not going to please you. No such generality occupies this whirring globe. But this will not stop me from discussing his function.

I believe that as we live, we gradually become aware that all things are not as we were led to believe, the most notable of these being the art of communication. How many times have you wondered whether you had made yourself clear? Should you be dealing with the question of buying groceries, perhaps many times, however with some experience of the laser eyes saying in their beams, 'Didn't I make it clear?' Perhaps not. Think then of the difficulty of trying to make your feelings of love clear to the object of your affection; or how you react to the 'Expulsion from Eden' of Massaccio; it is fearfully difficult for you to clarify these feelings even to yourself, never mind to others. I am convinced (as Rousseau was) that the factor that has separated man from his environment is the word. Yet language and the development of such is counted as one of his most remarkable achievements. In the word is founded man's arrogance. He has viewed the lack of words in the other natural world as a kind of stupidity and unworthiness which will preclude his serious consideration. He will not identify with his brother. How can he in his blindness have assumed that the word is final, concise and understandable, when the opposite is blindingly true. Man's assumed supremacy in the world is thus based on a total misunderstanding. 'In the beginning was the Word,' we are told in Genesis. This could not be further from my truth. If it is regarded as the Truth, then we can trace man's separation from God with the ensuing tide of original sin much farther back than Eve and her golden delicious.

21

I consider that the aim of life is to get as close to the Source of Love as possible. If you have chosen this Source to be a thing called God, and if you consider this thing to be formless, nameless, a void, but nevertheless a void in which there echo unseen, half-perceived, misty voices of archetypal love and goodness, then it seems clear that the closer you approach, the less there is to say – or, better, the less that can be said. I will approach God in silence, with no thought, no action, nothing for the NO-THING. This idea leaves the most prized creations of man in an extremely full doss-house on the road to perception. Under this belief everything laid down by Mozart, Michael Angelo, Bach, Bellini (Giovanni) etc, etc, are cries of misunderstanding or barely-comprehended bliss. There is an argument to release us from this fog and this is to assume that all offerings are in praise of the being. God in my vision needs nothing and gives nothing. He exists for us to pluck at with our often too short arms, but for every piece of edible love plucked from beneath the carapace two will fill the space. Thus love is inevitable and inexorable and ultimately will cover us and drown us. This state can only occur when the desire of self, control, doing good and all 'isms' are extirpated. In this Elysium there will be no need of propaganda with which the less than intellectually tough are kept in a worldly thrall, and the love of God falls into the rapacious paws of career politicians often masquerading in dog-collars, or self-uneasy saints acting the roles of caring psychiatrists. 'Thy will be done' seems to me to be the most ignored part of the Lord's Prayer.

22

I have wandered again, but now I will come clean. Having uttered the old cliché 'It spoils your breakfast but not your lunch' many times, I now freely admit that criticism bothers me. It's not that I particularly dislike being lauded or castigated. This is not my problem. It lies rather in a moral zone. I have never understood the function of criticism. Let me discuss its accepted *raison*, coolly and objectively. It could be said that it can aid a somnolent public to awareness in the art of its time. It may be said that it serves to support standards in painting, literature and music, thus safeguarding those standards. It can be said that it fills theatres and galleries and likewise the bank balances of actors, managers, artists and dealers. It must certainly be said that it fills many newspapers and other publications with its print.

Today, the 18th September, I bought a heavy Sunday paper (I honestly cannot remember the one even at six hours' distance) and read the words of the music critic. He told me without doubt and in great detail why *Falstaff* at the Welsh National Opera was ineffably wonderful and that *La Traviata* at the English National Opera was woeful. For some minutes I found myself reading as if I were in the presence of fact and having seen neither production, I was closely acquainted with both.

I had become a victim of propaganda. I would try and see the one, but not the other. It was not too long, however, before I realised the enormity not only of what had happened to me, but also to all those singers, musicians, also the audiences, also the public who read papers. We had accepted these words and had become the fodder of propaganda because we had chosen to ignore some basic self-evident truths. The first of these (and this is the moment when I hear the knockings on the inside of my deathly wooden horse)

that no word can convey what was really felt by the
writer (here we are back with words again) because I
reiterate that words themselves are ambiguous, crude
and general. Each word carries so much ambiguity
that it is only possible to interpret it quite selfishly,
this being based on early experiences and individual
shadows. Ergo, if the word green is mentioned by a
critic we only have a generalised idea of the colour
of which he is speaking. He was convinced of what
he saw, but how can we share the obvious insularity
of his experience and soul? So not only is every word
suspect and misunderstandable but so is his spirit which is even more complex, his past learnings,
hurts and pleasures. How can I become privy to his
accumulated experience? Even if this were possible,
how much nearer would I be to understanding him?
Should I think I had, I still could not escape my own
eyes' vision of him. This is a double bind, at least.
Everything we read we cannot truly understand but
still we idly settle for quarter-truths and think – no,
not only think, but believe we have understood.

It really must be a very difficult job to sustain.
Imagine what it entails; the obstacles to be faced.
You must go out to yet another concert leaving a
warm burning fire dancing with images. On goes the
coat and you begin your struggle with the mad world
outside. You never wanted to hear or see the play but
it's part of your load. It is a boring concert, you think
the players, the singers rotten. What do you do? You

must write something. You write something not too hurtful because you are a nice man and proceed to phone it to an idiot at the other end of the line who can't distinguish between Meredith and Mère Edith. You go back home to a dead fire and prepare for tomorrow's day. As you fade into a fitful sleep a devil reminds you that those awful performers were probably paid fifty times as much for their evening's caper as you were.

'And don't forget you're the one with the brains,' insists little Lucifer. Little Lucifer is soon transformed into Big Nick the Elder who, recognising vulnerable flesh, begins to poke at it most unpleasantly.

'Then what do you think of your function?' He is now the interrogator.

'What, when the evening of the morning is come, do you consider your achievement?'

He answers in pragmatic terms, he must earn a living, perhaps he does some good, he certainly saves people wasted journeys and pounds.

Beelzebub continues.

'Obviously, you must understand,' he says ironically, 'that a comment on an event past and gone is a pure waste of effort. If it is not so, then you are still trying to influence generations to come concerning an event that can only be ephemeral. You say you help a singer to perfect his art,' the devil continues, his tail twitching, obviously warming to his subject. 'Every artist is his own best critic. He knows his every deficiency. He knows how horrible he is. He is disappointed ninety-five per cent of the time. The remainder occurs when everything is correct and working; energy, technique, health, involvement; and he is inordinately pleased. If your vision and his do not correspond then the conclusion to be drawn is that you both started out on different lines which never found a junction.'

He continues: 'A question which has often beguiled me is why you write your critiques for people who could not possibly have attended the event.'

The critic begins to answer but is not quick enough. Before he speaks, follows: 'You also give the impression that in some way you are an "expert" in your field. "Expert" in the field of art usually describes the highjacking of a little-known artist by a visual entrepreneur. He adds a pinch of academic tract to his capture and flogs himself to the auctioneers who depend on him, thereafter, wholly for their attributions. Criticism often appears to be the occupation of the academic on parole or the creative impulse on death row for need of a gift. I'm sure you'll agree.' Without pausing for breath, he goes on, 'For you simply must realise that your work is a "short cut" for those of weak intellect and idle will. They will read your piece and stay at home. You have prevented those voters from thinking, from realising their uniqueness. What you do, is to throw your blanket of genius or mediocrity over possibly positive souls. In depriving them of their judgment you deprive them

of their secret selves. You also deprive actors of many a full house should your review be negative. You do have great power. But I do not blame you.' He speaks so indulgently. 'I blame instead the indigent, half-interested, half-alive, half-intelligent one that is so besmirched with hubris that he bothers to read you.' Concluding: 'And where would the smart dinner-party be without you? Without the received opinion from the morning rag, these jolly events would be conducted not in the dining-room but in a sepulchral vault, or perhaps even the Sistine Chapel where that ferocious little man rushes at anyone suspected of whispering.'

23

Critics do indeed have a great influence, especially in the corridors of taste in our national institutions. This influence is not often direct, but more subtle, slipping neatly into the crevices of the less than certain opinion. The English are generally suspicious of professionals. The enthusiastic amateur is their choice. There is a certain Corinthian grandeur associated with flawed debonair obsession. Consequently many of the boards of directors of our institutions, and I speak more nearly of the Royal Opera House as I know a little of the place, are peopled by high professionals from other fields, but amateurs in music. The membership of the board tends to be a reward for great duty and skill in these other fields. There is not one singer on the board at Covent Garden, nor a director. The conductor is included but as he is surrounded by business and career politicians he is generally outmanoeuvred. So having no credentials for criticism other than those of the general public, they rely (cantankerously, it seems to me) on the paid arbiters. When they make their report on a certain performance, their opinions having been made for them, they regurgitate what I think I have already proved to be undigested misunderstandings. So the critical influence reaches into the slowly-beating heart of authority.

'The Heroic Symphony contains much to admire, but it is difficult to keep up admiration of this kind during three long quarters of an hour. It is infinitely too lengthy. . . . If this symphony is not by some means abridged, it will soon fall into disuse.' *The Harmonicon*, London, April 1829.

'Berlioz, musically speaking, is a lunatic, a classical composer only in Paris, the great city of quacks. His music is simply and undisguisedly nonsense. He is a kind of orchestral Liszt, than which I could name nothing more intensely disagreeable.' *Dramatic Musical Review*, London, January 7th, 1843.

'The music of *Le Sacre du Printemps* baffles verbal

description. To say that much of it is hideous as sound is a mild description. There is certainly a compelling rhythm traceable. Practically it has no relation to music at all as *most* of us *understand* the *word.' Musical Times*, London, August 1st, 1913.

(By the way, Beelzebub italicised the three words in the last quotation.)

I do not want to appear grouchy, bitter or red-necked concerning the critical function, but I find it impossible to say anything in its favour. As to the people who work at it, I can only respect them when they do something proper. David Cairns is a notable man, I believe. He keeps a fine distance from personal comment, talks passionately about the philosophic motor which propels music, and above all writes brilliantly and fully about the great Berlioz. Still this can't absolve a breed which steadfastly wishes a daffodil were a tulip, stubbornly refuses to alter preconception at the instant, and bewails that a pig is not a hippopotamus. So saying, this subject is boxed up. I may open the box again. I'm not sure yet.

24

I will now tell you of the worst experience (musical) of my life so far. The scene was to be set at Covent Garden, the occasion Dame Janet Baker's farewell stage performance. The work was *Alceste* of Glück. Janet has spoken at some length of this event in her book, but as a very important player in this drama I feel that I should give my account. The rehearsals, five weeks in all, had passed off remarkably well. One of the weekends had been set aside for me to make a journey to Cardiff to film a television programme. The driver arrived for me early in the morning, having already driven the distance from Cardiff. His brief was to come for me, take me, bring me back and then, return. Quite a task, I thought. We had a non-eventful trip (apart from my having to be a little sharp with the driver who, it seemed, wanted to chain-smoke for two and a half hours), followed by a non-eventful television recording. We finished early, and this is where I first learned of the chauffeur's task. There he was, fag in hand, waiting for me and looking a mite tired, I thought. We set out. As I had been in the company of this man for too long already, I feigned sleep and sank myself deep into the back seat. About an hour along the way came a frightful thump and I found myself thrown down into the well between front and back seats. The driver, almost comatose when awake, I presumed had fallen asleep. The car had hit the one in front, swerved round and was left facing the oncoming traffic in the fast lane of M4 east-bound. By some amazing chance there was nothing behind us and we managed to reach the safety of the hard shoulder. We got out and my driver began to light up while petrol poured from his stricken car. I waited for an hour for my angel of mercy, Hilly, to rescue me. I was shocked, it was cold and so was I. It was a Sunday.

On Tuesday at rehearsal I noticed those familiar tell-tale needles. I enquired whether I was covered or not for the shows (a cover is an understudy). I was informed that someone was covering the part but had not yet memorised it. Not a lot of comfort. The days snailed on and my condition worsened with them, as did my hysteria. The familiar dark tunnel now began to constitute itself. Slowly I was being detached from the world. I take to the bath frequently in times of such stress (I suppose that this must be an attempt to return to the secure world of the womb). Life was not only boring and painful but terribly monotonous. The dark tunnel leads to the bath in which you cannot stay because the dark tunnel needs you. The world is tiny and stupid, the once-free soul is now the size of a withered walnut. People are now encumbrances to our worry, sleep a twisted dream, the journey to the Opera House accompanied by the tumbrils of the train. So arrived the dreaded, hideous day and with leaden soul and shackled feet I went to work. I must also mention that Hilly had been doing her keep-fit exercises in the kitchen. I heard a whip-crack which for a second punctured my adamantine world, followed by a cry for help. She had shattered a tendon and could not walk. Sticks became manifest.

I arrived at the Opera House and went straight to a room in 45, a building opposite the main house, to warm up what precious little voice I had. This would not do. With a gale behind me I might just be heard in the seventh row. I dared not put any pressure on the voice for fear of upsetting its already teetering balance, and compounding its infection. With a dreadful coldness of negation upon me only minutely warmed by the match heat of hope, I went to my dressing-room looking at, but not seeing my feet, and ignoring all my fit colleagues. My deep neurosis even prevented me from wishing Janet Toi-Toi. (This is a German form of *merde, in bocca lupo*, break a leg. It is the first part of *Teufel* – Devil.)

Admete, my role, plays no part in the first act so I had yet more time for my hysteria to begin not only to consume my soul but also to suck noisily at my brain. The interval between act 1 and 2 was of an indescribable horror. I was buffeted to madness in a vortex of despair.

Act two starts. In ten minutes I'm on. The bells ring, 'Act two beginners, please, Dame Janet, Mr Tear. . . .' I walk to the stage which looks physically like a necropolis. I will die here, I thought. I mount the Grecian stairs. I enter from on high. My first phrase, 'O mes enfants, O mes amis' lies in the middle of my range. With an expansive gesture I sing, or rather I try. Frighteningly little appears. The next phrase is a little higher and I now know without any doubt that I have about five notes that are working and these at a whisper and piteous. I go terribly, terribly cold, analytical, nihilistic. The dreadful gloom is lifted and I see with a hawk-like eye and understand with a crystal clarity, and know what I must do. It begins with an improvisation of genius around the five notes that I have. Janet's eyes are like saucers, her bewilderment complete, her jaw reattaches itself and she sings for me as the great colleague she is.

At the interval I told Sir John Tooley that my understudy should go on. He informed me that the part was still not memorised and therefore he couldn't. The dreadful – perhaps the worst – outcome was that he sang it from the pit and I mimed. It must have been ludicrous. This was indeed the deepest pit that I had yet visited. I must tell you that this charade was played out in front of the highly singular first night audience (naturally, as it was the first night). These people, or rather many of these people, arrive as late as possible and never properly sit down in case they might miss a glimpse of a new liaison or a new dress embarked upon or worn by their peers, or indeed be missed by them. The applause is at once polite and glovedly muted. Hilly dragged her painful stick-supported leg to the car and we went home. My mood was one of shock and intense relief.

The rider to this story (which also appears in Susie and Meirion Harries's book) is that two days later while watching television, I went blind in my left eye, which lasted for half-an-hour. Such can be the physical reaction to tension, and such can be the glamour of my profession.

25

I meant to tell you some time back, that I am inordinately fond of low-pressure systems. These mean to me, especially in winter, no fogs, ease of access, no cancellations, no loss of fees. I know that all this shrieks out against my philosophy, but it is the truth. However much money can be collected, it can never be enough to fight off the ides of future depressions and want. I suppose that this idiocy has its origins in my early life. Although all five of us lived in a council house we were never poor. My beatific granny Elsie kept a minute general shop in a disused guardsman's hut at the Buttrills, my father was a clerk for God's Wonderful Railway. My grandfather brought home money from the docks. The fact that Elsie used to wash the floors at the Grammar School was nothing to do with need, I think. I could be completely wrong. In any case, my feeling of financial insecurity is my own and will always be. So when the wind blows the leaves in my face and the rain batters my pate I feel at love with the world. It is the quiet sunny winter day that calls forth my fears, and those moony nights with tinkling frosts that remind me of fogs and lost fees.

26

I am now flying between Paris and Turku, that small beautiful old capital of Finland. Last night was a miracle. I sang, even to my ears, a stunning Herod at the Palais Garnier in Paris, and retired to bed. (By the way, I haven't told you that the acoustic in the Garnier is the best in Europe – the Coliseum, however, could well be its equal. I feel I could go straight back on and sing through the whole part again whatever it is; now because the political ego must triumph they are building a new one at the Bastille and giving the stupendous acoustic to the hoofers.)

I was awakened by the usual knell of death, hot eyes and catarrh (*vert solide*) rivetted to the back of the throat. This *botschaft* of evil woke me at 4.00. Sleep was impossible among the hot sweats. I sit looking down on Sweden, every lake a diamond catching the sun's gaudy eye. But I begin again to feel myself a leper – What if? What then? Let me stamp on all this nonsense and call insecurity a liar. So what! So! Nevertheless, should ever suicide be an alternative it could only be effected with the help of that strong, knotted noose of entwined writhing germs placed neatly on the inside of the neck.

27

Here's Caruso again:

'As regards eating – a rather important item, by the way – I have kept to the light "Continental" breakfast which I do not take too early; then a rather substantial luncheon towards two o'clock. My native macaroni, specially prepared by my chef, who is engaged particularly for his ability in this way, is often a feature in this mid-day meal. I incline towards the simpler and more nourishing food, though my tastes are broad in the matter, but lay particular stress on the excellence of the cooking, for one cannot afford to risk one's health on indifferently cooked food, no matter what its quality.

'On the nights when I sing I take nothing after luncheon, except perhaps a sandwich and a glass of Chianti, until after the performance, when I have a supper of whatever I fancy within reasonable bounds ... The continual effort of loud talking in a throng would be extremely bad for the sensitive musical instrument that the vocalist carries in his throat, and the various beverages offered at one of your afternoon teas it would be too difficult to refuse. So I confine myself to an occasional quiet dinner with a few friends on an off night at the opera, or an evening at the play, where I can at least be silent during the progress of the acts.

'After reading the above the casual person will perhaps believe that a singer's life is really not a bit of a sinecure, even when he has attained the measure of his world's approval and applause afforded by the "great horseshoe".'

28

Now, sitting draped around my neck a tabby cat whose name is Bruce (strange coincidence), says: 'You simply must have had wonderful experiences on stage when the wind was behind and both light and mind were inclined?'

My razor-sharp intellect informs me that this cat has joined my menagerie from the performances of *Salomé* in Paris. Lavelli the producer in his infinite wisdom has set the opera after the final cataclysm (no pun intended). The world is no more except for furry felines. Needing symbols of authority, Herod and Herodias have killed just enough of them for a coat each. They have stitched them together, ears and tails and legs and backs. I had been wearing one of these coats. I tried in vain to imagine its being accepted in England. It was pretty revolting, I confess. Anyway, one of these cats has assumed a powerful resurrection and feeling unduly guilty because of my implied cooperation in and with the unseemly coat, I answer him.

'Yes, they are countless and if I could even begin to write the count-down the world would quickly run out of ink. But ever in such a treasure-house (the cellars and the attics too are full) certain greater moments stand out from the rest.'

The first would be the Choral Scholarship that I sang for Boris Ord at King's. The sight-singing for a raw Grammar School lad of seventeen was fierce enough, but the tiger-skin rug with head horribly alive and maw gaping with shining ivory teeth was fiercer and a true test of concentration. When I had finished my song (Benedictus – Mass in B minor) in the Chapel, Doctor Ord came up to me and said: 'Have you had any singing lessons, Mr Tear?'

'No, Sir,' I replied.

'Good!' he said. 'Then you won't ruin my choir.'

Then there was the only audition I performed at; I was temperamentally unsuited to these things, being naturally unwilling to perform well under the conditions set by others, when Solti engaged me to sing Lensky at Covent Garden. This was indeed my second role at the house and since then I have performed at least three hundred and fifty times as a guest artist. But these were beginnings, leanings. I remember almost every date with huge affection. One I remember with blinding recall was the David (*Meistersinger*) I sang at Covent Garden conducted by Colin Davis. (By the by, he is to my mind the most widely intelligent of all the conductors I have worked with.) The list of modes that David sings is one of the most beautiful pieces of music ever written for the voice. It is like the most wonderfully orchestrated long song. It lasts about twenty-five minutes and is rather like a concerto for voice and orchestra. All action stops while David recites these modes and tones. At one performance there was such a stupendous understanding between Colin and me, that neither of us had to look or even care. It was as if the music was being thrown back and fore on an endless subtle rubber band of imagination. Nothing could be dropped or damaged. The orchestra felt this careless collaboration and of course were one with us.

A similar experience happened to me quite recently. I was rehearsing a new *Das Rheingold* in Munich. We had arrived at the first stage and orchestra, which as I have said before, is always quite a tense affair as the conductor (Sawallisch) expects all your attention and the producer wants you to carry out all the moves previously rehearsed for the past five or six weeks with feeling. Immediately I began to sing I knew that nothing could go wrong. Sawallisch smiled once and we began to play the most satisfying musical games. Such moments are indeed magical and eclipse completely those tensions of performances when the body, or rather my body, is not quite up to it.

As an afterthought I must say that Colin Davis, with two extremely good pieces of advice, has had a tremendous influence on my musical development. The first, 'Never stop a note until its whole length has been sung,' and second, 'Never portamento up and always down.' Also his conducting style, as that of Georg Solti, has influenced me greatly.

I would say that Loge is my favourite role. It is the most intelligent of parts. He stands without the idiocies of the Gods and all characters, he returns in *Götterdämmerung* and destroys the whole edifice with his fire. He is half God, half man, rather like us all. It's not that he's malicious in the slightest, though it must be admitted that he shows pique when the full Gods are crumbling, before he and Wotan travel to Nibelheim. In a strange way his character represents truth and, in an intellectual way, love. He is not just logic, he is parted from this Newmanian mid-glory and has joined the reality of loneliness, temperament and God. It is because of the fact that it *is* in his nature and without control that he finally destroys the bourgeois and political antics of the Gods who surround him. The music is magically written, like chamber music, with subtleties at every turn. Wagner never writes too heavily for the voice, everything is balanced in perfection. The vocal line is melodic, romantic, sardonic, sarcastic, parlando, infinitely singable, elegant, sharp. It is neither too high nor too low. All concentration might therefore be channelled into the playing of this very subtle demi-God.

29

I may speak of some other roles later, but now I feel that I should tell you something of the Pauline bolt that hammered me on the busy road to nowhere. (At this moment, the cat, who was quite intrigued for a while, fell from my shoulders in boredom, in a similar way as I hear dull thuddings of books hitting floors, carpets and duvets, now falling from sleeping hands. He fell to earth heavily, breaking his neck on a stone cat that we keep on the hearth warming his lifeless body against a fire that very rarely burns. This was his tenth and last chance. Good riddance, I say, a resurrected cat with hubris, who ever heard of it? Requiescat (Oh! Oh, dear!) in Pace, Bruce.

30

I am a quiet admirer of inconsistency. It disrupts that
comfort which tends to make people feel that they are
permanent. This comfort tends to close their eyes to the
living vibrant seconds as they rush by. Inconsistency
can awake them and can activate a torpid soul. Now
remember what I said concerning the word? Remember the theorising? I still believe it completely when
speaking of the ideal world where mind cuffs would
not be the rule. But cop this one.

Iris Murdoch once said that 'the search is a love-
affair'. The search has also been my appointed task
and the affair also mine. I have not mentioned before
that my granny used to call me a useless 'omidore'.
I continued to occupy this indefinable noun; no one
has yet translated it. I married my Hilly in 1961 and
remained omidorised. Why such a smashing young
creature wished to be bound to such a vaporous soul
I have no idea and I'm fairly certain she had none. I
admit that I had always felt 'religious' impulses and
filled my vacant mind for several vacant hours with

musings on the nature of good and love and evil with, it must be admitted, positively negative results. So feeling in need of amusement or more nearly from desperation, I walked into a shop in Notting Hill Gate, walked aimlessly to the book counter, mindlessly raised my hand, with no thought gripped a paperback between my opposable thumb and index digit and withdrew a book on Buddhism by Christmas Humphreys. In a flash I was rendered a quivering, seeking, neo-happy wreck, proto half-baked saint. Scales fell from my eyes (Billingsgate was a corner shop) and clattered, leaping and jumping, fell again to rise to fall, filling the air with the sounds that dead skin dropping to earth would make to a bat. The tympany of 1812 would have been useless and inadequate in comparison. This was what I was meant for (had I been meant for anything, this was the bit that had been in refrigeration, these were the darkened rooms, and this was the switch). Books mostly by Alan Watts followed, most notably a masterpiece entitled *The Wisdom of Insecurity*. This is a book which has such force of intellectually-organised belief and such difficult honesty that it sends running for cover those incestuous academic philosophers who play games with words purely for the territory of academe. I realised that I had needed a religion (for need of a more subtle word) in which I was not forced to go on living for ever. So silver pieces covered gold until nothing covered even more nothing. No-thing or God or good or love would not be by-passed. It did not exist for me, but I for It. The case for disproving God now became impossible. I certainly required no personal God, at least not one who viewed me from afar with gigantic opera glasses and cared for me like a benevolent headmaster. I knew that something was making a determined knocking on the box of my soul.

I am a reasonably welcoming chap and I opened the door of my soul and enquired who was beating so insistently. A voice answered: 'I am the void.' I beckoned this void into my soul but there was little room for the both of us. I mentioned this and was answered that there were not two of us but three. To my enquiry the void said, 'You are not one but two; your eternal soul and your posturing ego. Throw away the one and there will be room for me.' I was faced with a choice of throwing away all that seemed to be me, self, position, pride, security, decisions, lust, for the seemingly quiescent areas of acceptance, waiting, detachment, general love without discrimination. Would I take a fast leap from the high cliff of seeming security into the abyss of the unknowing, or partake in an elegant but increasingly vapid walk around and around the confines of the intellect and vaunting ego. I chose the valley of death (as it seemed then), the wilderness, black without shape.

Accept that at this moment, at the age of twenty-three, I was first born. From then, I had the possibility of true freedom (not that of the mouth, which is so concerned with rights. If you see God what is there to say,

94

what need of rights?) Good was suddenly a dominant force that would be ignored at my peril. This peril was the separation from good. Good was God and the both were life, the time spent from them was a waste of life which in fact was death. Thus logically evil was death. I was left happily lonely and gloriously loitering.

But it also led me into even more lonely areas of morality. When does caring become a charabanc full of egos? *Of course* we are all the same and all different and *of course* we are diminished when anything dies. But also (*of course*) how can we tell when people die that we cannot know of. Our love surely, practically, must only be directed to those we can see or know or touch. We cannot love a mankind we cannot comprehend. Politicians and the professional religious will try and make us do this, but that is really because they need to organise and control. All politicians must control in their own names and egos. If man does not attempt control, he will tend to believe that he does not exist, will find himself lonely in a world he does not understand, speaking a language he does not comprehend. All organised religions, governments, mothers' unions, boy scouts spring to life to gainsay the natural solitariness of the soul, and all have within them the seeds of the desire to control or sometimes the desire not to be controlled. It is even impossible to be an anarchist because the very classification of this idea renders it followable and thence political.

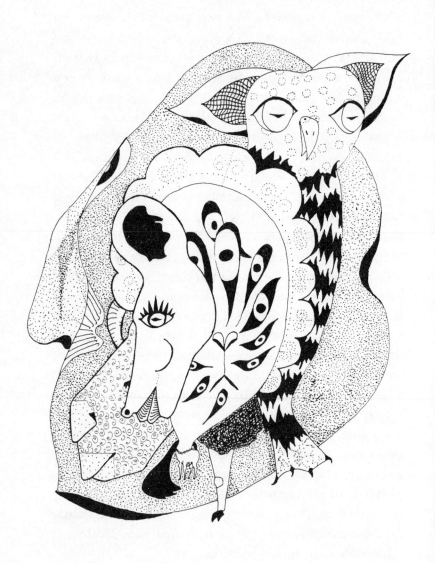

31

It would please me now to talk of other things. I fully realise that the dark spirit constantly waits to taunt me with self-love, arrogance and all self-defeating things, but I am ready for him, fully armed with eyes open.

This time I won't speak of things musical or spiritual. I now consider another blissful summer's day when true fantasy was made blazingly manifest. I will now give a precis of my sporting prowess. As a Welsh boy it was not enough (as I said previously) to be a success with the voice or the brain; one had also to be seen to be a success in manly sports. I had tried rugby and was good when I was twice the size of the other lads. Soon, however, they caught up and I began to find the game unpleasantly dangerous, and one day, coming up from a tackle with grass sticking out of my front teeth like some demented ruminant, I decided enough was certainly enough. Cricket was my next target. I was moderately successful at this and also immoderately nervous, being violently sick before every game for fear that I would let the others down. This, although I did not know it at the time, was the most nervous I was ever to get. I was a correct defensive batsman with a decent square cut and deft nudges to leg. I couldn't drive at all, I remember. I was sufficiently decent to be given the final trial for a cap for Wales. I opened the innings with Tony Lewis (later to captain England) and had the immense distinction of scoring precisely five runs in the same time as it took him to score seventy-five. Having not unduly troubled the scorers, my cap was, not surprisingly, not forthcoming. At Cambridge I played soccer for King's, lurking in the centre-forward position and scoring some goals. The only problem with this was that I always had to leave the field early in order to get to evensong. Sometimes when I squelched off we were 3–1 up, only to lose in the last quarter of an hour. Apart from tennis, which I took up later, as you know, that was that. I did like sport, it must be said. I was well co-ordinated and strong, big enough and filled with just enough desire to win, or if this was not possible, at least to make my opponent(s) sweat. (This feeling of general bloody-mindedness was engendered, I believe, by thousands upon thousands of futile draughts games played against my father, not one of which I ever managed to win. I became bloody but not bowed.) Almost every Saturday I have sat before the TV gawping at sport. This I now realise was a deeply selfish act and I apologise to my dear family in retrospect.

One day I came home from work and Hilly said,

out of the cliché-ed blue:

'Would you like to play cricket against Ian Botham and Somerset?'

In a strange way the question was almost meaningless. Had she said, 'Would you like a frame of billiards against Bruce Mozart or would you like to hand Vincent his brushes and then carefully clean them?' I shouldn't have believed her. But this question beggared my intellect and left me white and dumb. Would I clip God's toenails? Of course, of course I would. A natural sycophant in presence of greatness and also an ego-centric swine (except in the terms aforementioned), it took me some time and the odd sleepless night to regain my equilibrium. The second part of this word would have been useful, had I any to hand. Sleep was eventually so fugitive that huge haversacks (remember them, the stigmata marks of the thirties) hung below my eyes. Ancient bats with worm were oiled and young lads dragooned into turning over their ever-eager arms. The day, when it eventually arrived, was a thoughtless idiot of perfection, the odd wispy half-imagined cloud floating aimlessly across a sun that burnt ever so gently and a slow breeze that abetted it. It was a small, beautiful ground in Bath close-bordered by the Avon.

I was part of a Celebrity team, that was engaged, as I said previously, to play Somerset, thank God without Richards and Garner who were on tour with the Windies. Among our strength I would name an exceptional cricketess, and England international called Sarah Potter (daughter of the playwright). Of the rest we flourished a painter, a writer (Leslie Thomas) and the playmaker Tom Stoppard, behind the timber. Against us was assembled the county riding swiftly for the championship. I remember vividly a few neatly selected events. The first was of my old dad who made the trip from Wales specially for the match. We sank some happy pints together. The second was of a glazier standing with quick pride in front of his work. He stole a quicker word with the lady of the house, looked back and saw a ball struck by the greatest cricketer of our time shattering his creation. The third was the vision of this hero competing with vigour against us maggots. There was a bottle of champagne for the man that could hit the smartest fifty. Martin Crowe was leading but Botham had to win. At the end of the game, instead of opening the bottle in the more accepted manner, he knocked the neck off it in wild west fashion, cut his finger and missed the next test match. The final memory is frozen in sepia for all time in my grateful memory. Sarah bowled, Botham's bat flashed and standing on the long on boundary with short eyes and also minding my own business, an intuition warned me that the ball was homeing in on me. If I saw it, I saw it late. For a fraction of a second I saw a red blur wheeling just right of me not rising or falling but continuing inexorably towards me. The sound I heard was of eagles' wings. A hard object struck my hands, causing internal bleedings, and dropped to the sward. The sound of groaning and sorrow was heard in that pleasant land. Shoes fell over Edom.

Sarah said, 'Had you caught it, that would have been the greatest day of my life.' How little she knew me. Had I caught it my apotheosis would have been eloquent, colourful and notable. As for the grimy facts. He scored two hundred, I bowled six overs, dismissing the wicketkeeper Garde and was only hit for one six by the presence. I hit him for three to square leg before becoming cocky hitting across his ever-growing venomous line and being bowled.

32

It has been my great fortune to live and sing at the same time that two great composers were building their notes. It would be remiss of me, I think, if I did not say something of my collaboration with them. I refer, naturally, to Benjamin Britten and Michael Tippett. You might well have thought that the bestiary which insolently appears without bidding in these pages, was a clever ruse to stimulate conversation and pose questions that would look dull if not voiced in speech. This is only part of the truth. The other part, and please do not ask me to quantify it, is that these creatures personify rebellious legions of my psyche. One of the reasons for my harbouring these virulent mercenaries is my early relationship with B. B. You might well think that all the creatures are either dead or forgotten. They mostly are, it is true. One, however, remains and it sits, a beautiful devil with glorious translucent metallic powder-blue wings, very near to me, wherever I am. As I begin to think of those old old days in the stable at Aldeburgh ('silly old potato' Ben called Beethoven), my devil seems ever more malleable and sweet. He listens, amused with honest interest. Pray God he will fly and leave this man for good. Perhaps I mean ever.

33

It was years ago when I got off the train at Thorpeness Halt. This was not so much a station as a shack one sees in Western flicks. I walked under gloomy lowering Suffolk skies into a bitter wind and asked of the first Indian I saw the whereabouts of the working men's club. I was directed to a wooden structure, more dead man's gulch than England. As I entered the hall I felt a strange atmosphere around me, and knew that the sanctuary I had entered was weird, personal, unhealthy, obsessive, perhaps incestuous, but above all these, seductive. All seemed at gentlemanly rest and nothing was. There was unrest, unhappiness in the air, secrecy in the grain of the wood. Politeness kneaded the place with whistling claws. Manners were perfect, care was offered with hooded talons. I was new and very afraid. My clean antennae twitched and received messages of secrecy and shadow. In those days my intuition, I promise you, did not deceive me. My first impression remains like a first state Rembrandt etching, clear, brilliantly clear with sharp differential in every stroke. It remains through the years. That was 1963 and today is a day in September 1988, and I still feel the oddness of it. Still I feel the perfect outsider. I had been invited to a dinner of mysterious half tastes – meat, half fish, fruit – part animal, toxic drink. I almost exaggerate.

I had been engaged to cover Peter Pears in the first performance of *Curlew River*, the first of the church operas.

Where should I begin with Britten? From those early days when my feelings for him were so ambiguous (between hero worship and active dislike) and I thought his music mere illustration, or from these slightly more mature days when I consider him a great composer but still have to balance this greatness with perceived cruelty?

I remember so many cruelties apart from those concerning me. The famous remark that 'I'm very disappointed with your work, you're using my music as a vocal exercise,' three minutes before I went on, was only one. When recording the *St John Passion*, that fearful aria *'Ach mein Sinn'*, he obviously was not overpleased with me and said, 'Well, if that's all you can do, you'd better go on doing it.' When Viola Tunnard, who was beginning to be afflicted with motor-nerve disease, was told when offering to step down from the harpsichord in *Idomeneo*, 'You'd better stay, we've tried everybody else and no one is free.' I remember the weekends people were kept waiting before they were told if they were sacked or not. I remember above all the terrible atmosphere of Aldeburgh – an atmosphere laden with waspishness, bitterness, cold, hard eyes, with cabalistic meetings under the Cherry Tree with Pimms, with the inscrutability of the elite. It was an atmosphere of secrecy.

However I remember those times when Ben was so wonderfully charming that when he spoke to me the world seemed to stop. What great games of table-tennis we had. He would serve wicked, but quite illegal spins, and said to me once, 'Remember, Bob, you will never beat the composer.' Sometimes his comments were so odd that they could only be excused by thinking them ironic. Once, when dressed in the stone make-up and wig for the male chorus in *The Rape of Lucretia* I had also put on some chic easy-rider dark glasses for a joke, and walked out into the corridor in the Maltings – when I say walk, I think I mean mince – singing that hideous line, 'With you two arm-in-arm again, Rome can sleep secure,' in a very queeny way and bumped straight into Ben. He appeared very angry and said, 'This is hardly the way to treat my grand opera.'

He was without doubt the greatest musician I have ever met. His piano playing had more clarity and point than any I have heard. I think it must be admitted that when he played Schubert for Peter the songs (because of his huge personality) did sound remarkably like Britten: but his insight was peerless. He was the greatest conductor I have worked with. His secret, I think, was a covered insistence of tempo. All passion was kept just out of sight under a warmish blanket of control. His music always moved on. No note ever died, but was activated by his personal irritation or lack of comfort. Forward however was hidden. But nothing rested content. I think now I look back, that my chief impression of Ben was of a man in terminal irritation, an irritation clearly of himself. His conducting technique was imperfect, but no one cared when the music was fired with such inner passion – I should like to say anger, I can't go that far, but I also won't say love.

Thinking of him as a composer I still find myself compromised. Without doubt he was the greatest illustrator of a text since Purcell. He even was able to add stature to already incomparable verse. I can think of no more perfect setting of the Shakespeare sonnet 'When most I wink'. Here the drama of a relationship is brought screamingly into focus, the hopelessness of communication lit brightly. I can think of no greater creation of atmosphere than the first two bars of Cotton's 'The days grown old, the fainting sun'. Had Shakespeare had

the notes he could not have done better to illustrate
night magic than the glissando chords at the beginning of *Midsummer Night's Dream*. The grief of *Sinfonia
da Requiem* is tangible. And yet I am left wanting. This
obviously is nothing to do with Ben's huge gift but
rather with my temperament. Believing that innocence
can only be worked for and perhaps achieved during a
life, Ben's vision of a born perfect soul that will be cor-
rupted is inimical to me. Therefore the themes of most
of his operas I find unsympathetic. Also my vision of
the outsider as being all of us doesn't match with Ben's.
He believes that the world will mobilise against one that
doesn't conform. I believe that individually every man
cannot be categorised and is alone and cannot conform
except perhaps to the idiocy of pragmatic rules. Therefore I see every man as apart. The operas are brilliant
pieces of theatre, as expert as Puccini. He knows to
the second how to end a scene or make his point. *The
Turn of the Screw* is for my taste his most effective piece.
His most outrageously glamorous, *Billy Budd*. It was
most curious that as he became older and ill with his
heart his music began to lose its pulse. I believe that
this was in direct connection with his illness. As his
heart became more vulnerable and his pulse weaker,
so did his music. The church operas, as in some way
the masterpiece *Death in Venice*, are without onward
force. These are in huge contrast to the power and thrust
of *Grimes* and the force of his baton.

My biggest difficulty with Ben lies in his philosophy.

— — —

I'm not talking now of his obsessions with the outsider or the corruption of innocence. I'm talking on a wider scale. He has always seemed to me bourgeois in his thought. He took very few chances with accepted truths. Even in his greatest religious piece, the *War Requiem*, he doesn't rethink anything, but gives the old mass a new look by incorporating English texts (Owen) within it. The conventional English middle-class wisdom is his. Where Michael Tippett sees religion as a personal and individual quest – look for example at the huge canvas he paints in the *Mask of time* – Ben retires to the safe ground of the mass, Anglicanism commenting, if unconsciously, on his intellectual and spiritual quiescence. Finally I must say that I didn't find Ben and Peter to my taste. As I say this I hear a flapping of huge blue see-through wings as my personal Lucifer flies off, never to be seen again.

34

If you hope that my zoo is forever gone then you hope too soon, for I will speak this time of a dog. Please breathe again, this dog is a real one. This is a dribbling boxer dog. The whole thing happened so long ago that I sometimes believe that I must have dreamt it, but then a sharp memory tells me it's true.

The grand setting was Lincoln Cathedral, a building of super beauty and supernatural cold. Wrapped in coat against the ravaging wind and nine hundred years of rising damp, I prepared, standing on a box at the west end, to sing the most taxing and also the most religious section of the *Matthew Passion* of Bach.

'Then Peter remembered the words of Jesus, and he went out and wept bitterly.' To these words Bach affixes the most cruel line, going up to a high B on the word 'out' and then melismatically and sinuously writing a line of stupendous pain and power taking the poor tenor back to an A and finally in my case to an F sharp decrescendo.

I was just setting myself up for this Everest when at the far end of the nave in this vast and packed cathedral, I saw a movement, a scurrying, nervous movement. I could see not much more than an alert spot. This spot moved closer as did my fiendish section. Soon I could make it out. The bounce of a prick-eared boxer is unmistakable, a combination of bambi and bull.

'Then began he to curse and to swear.' Then began he to stop with intelligent eye and head cocked to the left, brightly, in front of my box. Then began he to regard me with even more wonder as the congregation began to view him with even more disrespect.

'Ere the cock croweth, thou shalt deny me thrice.' His attention and his theology was now a myriad steps higher than that of the people. Then at the most exquisite blending of registers, 'And he went out,' his love and interest were at their most acute. Unfortunately an ass (this time a black-backed verger) decided that enough was certainly that and that animals had no place in his church, made a dive at the dog, no doubt to capture and chastise his impudence. As God would have it, the ass's foot caught a chair-leg as his hand did the right hind leg of the dog. Down they both went in a whimpering, snarling mass and God entered man's cathedral in his grossest shape. The considered religious moment had been trumped by the real thing.

35

I have always found it extraordinary (as before said), how people will gather under any aegis to defer their separate loneliness. One of the most obvious of these occasions happens at Easter time at the Festival Hall in a performance of the *St Matthew Passion* conducted by the truly lovely David Willcocks (a great Bach conductor). At these performances the communal will tries to convert the ghastly space of the building into Chartres, Ely, Durham or St Mark's. It not only succeeds in doing this but does even better. From the stage it is almost possible to see Norman arches rise imperceptibly from the colourless seats, glorious architraves appearing but only slowly, and wisps of holy thought weaving and crotcheting from the communal mind. Here is imposed nationality, here is the ghost of misunderstood Elgar, here is the strength of Anglicanism (so vapid in argument), shown in suit and sandwich. If this comment appears to be cynical, it is not. It is the true heart of that bit of dear England and it is difficult not to get caught in its heaving pulse. This for a singer would be lethal and must be avoided at every point. But the truth of the herd remains and I would say, 'Go home, every one of you and consider your lonely deaths and when you know God also brings you pain, then praise him immoderately.'

36

A few years ago I was asked to write an article on Michael Tippett to honour his birthday. This I did. As my ideas have changed little since then I will quote it. Here it is.

A certain philosophy, a specially perceived aura, renders me a begging prey. In my early times, even before any desired form could be invented by my short intellect, my feelings were mysteriously inclined. Questions without answers were preferred – intuitions invariably warmed while certainties froze the cockles.

When a kind of maturity arrived and questionings could at least lead a hesitant way, I discovered that other people's writings and supposed feelings could be aligned with mine. Those people who feel a necessity to define the unutterable called these others 'mystics', or again to make dully plain, those who feel they have a one-to-one relationship with God, or however the observer could wish to define the feeling. The Saints Augustine and Francis played leading roles, Meister Eckhart and St John of the Cross no less. Thomas Traherne and Lao Tsu were the impresarios, Nietzsche the Feste of the piece, Blake the producer, Redon the designer, Vaughan Williams . . . but his pantheism fell a little short of my obsession. There could be only one composer to write my 'Magic Life' – he is Michael Tippett. Messiaen might have done, but in some way he flies too near authority. John Taverner the elder would have done, but I felt a certain commitment to living links in my blessed chain. Michael has provided my link to Blake, Palmer, Herbert, Quarles, Chesterton, Watts and many more, and I thank him and am grateful.

At frequent times during my singing life (which is now well past its jubilee) I have been faced with Tippett's notes. Sometimes these notes have been quite new waiting to be breathed into life; other times, older words have waited for the new other times, older notes have waited for the new interpretations that must arrive with new voices and thoughts. Michael has been a constant in my life. But with old and new I receive

a remarkably faithful impression. This is of breathless-
ness (I am now not talking of technique) and a feeling
of drunkenness and blessedness. I can be transported
so that I no longer occupy my usual area – the earth
recedes, the self fades away and security becomes an
idiocy. I remember that my first awareness of this
state was clearly perceived when I performed *The
Heart's Assurance*. The showers of notes in *O Journey-
man* and *The Dancer* quite overwhelmed me. When
the whirlings became too much, suddenly there was a
sunlit plain with Martinesque vistas – quiet, beautifully
sad music, but never sentimental. When I look back
and remember the wonderful soul-uprising figures in
Boyhood's End alongside the oft-voiced criticisms that
there are 'too many notes', I simply know that this
whirlwind of sound followed by areas of stillness is
essential to the mesmeric effect that Tippett achieves.
I remember sitting in a London Church, listening to
the *Western Wynde* mass of John Taverner (when I say
listening, I mean the battering of my head and soul by
whirls of eddying notes) and thinking that this is the
technique that frees the mind from its logical chains.
Michael Tippett well understands this phenomenon.

Michael tries for the impossible and at most times
he succeeds. The Nothing is clearly a difficult concept
to elucidate in any form. Words cannot do it for their
nature renders them concrete and misunderstandable.
Plastic art sometimes, almost by accident, achieves its
end. When nothing must be said, music finds itself in

the best position for saying it. It is abstract and ill-suited for political and even programmatic purposes. Programme music is a corruption of the medium, turning it into second-rate poetry. Mozart achieves the non-didactic truth without effort. He stands free, knowing nothing, telling all. Michael, in my terms, stands in a similar position. He cares deeply for the stupidities of pride and all that affect most men. He cares, writes, and yet remains as he must a watcher with a clearer eye. He views from above, benevolent, hawk-like tries to better our sense and love – and will always fail.

Michael has always remained optimistic, confident that things are shareable and in swift evolution must change. Therefore he has followed movements with avidity. Having taken on the transcendental in the *Double Concerto, Corelli Fantasia, The Midsummer Marriage* and *Boyhood's End*, he moves on to more political issues in *The Heart's Assurance*, a mixture of pseudo-political with historical timeless myth in *King Priam* (what a masterpiece) and then to the burning question of the sixties – sexual identity and acceptable morality in *The Knot Garden*, then further again to the so-called ideas of political freedom in the *Ice Break*, to return unbroken and uncorrupt to the innocence of the *Triple Concerto* and the *Mask of Time*. My reaction to this homecoming is a sigh of great relief. To my spiritually biased view I found the exercises that Michael took into the politico-care arena very disturbing. I condisered him a man, more than any other, to be able to communicate the 'eternal now' to us, quenching our mystic thirst and refilling our bowls. To see this paragon dealing with the 'instant now' in such sincere terms worried me greatly and warned of misunderstandings. However, he has returned to me and I am glad.

There has always been that difficult time when my chosen heroes become political, or rather take a political stance from their exalted unified positions. Blake, Tippett and Nietzsche never could have been 'political animals' because they were not, as most politicians seem to be, in spiritual exile, but were always in touch with their selfless ground. Their dealings with the arid soil of politics must be taken as a concern for the Good – selflessly, eagle-eyed always seeing what it is, yet separate in their loneliness. This is how I can accept *The Knot Garden*. Although it is inspired by *The Tempest*, it seems not to be bound in to the effect of the inexorable elements on man and his desire to be with them, but rather to deal in the instant relationships of people with little understanding of themselves, or indeed of the unity of their fragmental selves with time. This is *my* difficulty – Michael has no such difficulty. He sees and occupies. Yet as the base of his occupation there exists no self-love, no self-seeking, no wanting, but an understanding of, rather an acceptance of the inexplicable.

As to us performers, we occupy the most odd position. It is at once careless and responsible. Michael has never written for anyone in particular, never for any quirk of technique, never for any 'thank you'. He has always written his truth irrespective of those who might perform it. Not for him the close tailorship of Mozart or Britten but instead the straight donation of Beethoven. He has always enjoyed his music, sitting back content, immoderately happy. He has no fears. He has abandoned self and consequently self-doubt. I am sorry to take such an Eastern position, but cannot explain things otherwise. The best that Michael can say is, 'Take it, do it,' – we know he will rarely intervene. We are left with golden problems in our tarnished minds and throats.

The frequently aired criticism concerning the quality of the libretti, with their often sudden modernisms which are always a little passé, compared with the inspirational sounds, is easily answered. Do not separate, do not divide his work. Tippett is at all times a unity. His music and his word are one. Any autopsy will declare imperfections. What of the libretti of *Die Zauberflöte* or *Fidelio*? Tippett's words are on a higher level than these. What of Wagner with his endless alliterations in such a bourgeois concept? Michael, in spite of occasional prolixity, is trying to describe the unnameable – is concerned with the ultimate. Far too much is made of these so-called weaknesses.

Michael Tippett's music gives me the feeling of endless possible joy. Joy, however, to be grasped only under certain conditions. The freeing of the mind from

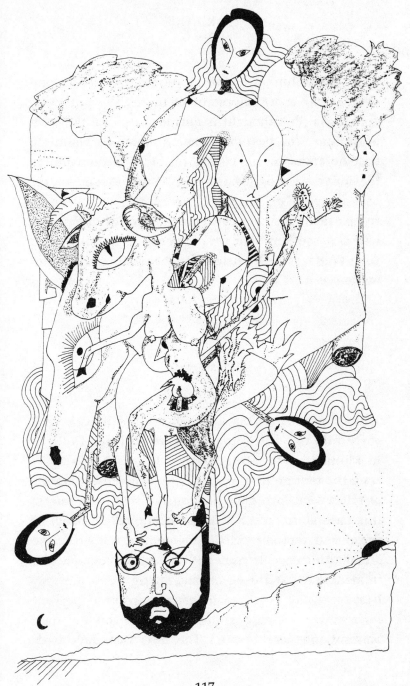

time and planning, the ability not to look before and after, is the most important of these. The gift to be able to see that thought is meant to conceal the truth is another. The best of Michael's music allows me to become more aware of my physical relationship to the universe and this is what I think is part of the true mystical experience. 'Life cannot be frozen or compartmentalised or conceptualised or even grasped. Life is something that simply keeps happening,' said Alan Watts. I thank Michael for the music which helps me to see it.

37

This is as close as the worst of the feeling can be. I am sitting in a small new room in the Hotel Dollman in Munich on the 29th March, 1987. Ten days ago I sang the first night of our *Ring* here after two months of rehearsals. Two days previously I had been caught in a snowstorm and had suffered immediate pangs of dread and remorse. At the moment of the first flake I had threatened myself with a sickness which had immediately fixed itself on me, falling from that grey heaven. (Why is snow in certain areas so perfect? I remember walking quite naked in it on my high balcony the year before.) The next two days were spent in a bed heavy with sweat. I bored my Hilly and teased her with my fear. Then Lazarus-like I arose and sang a fine show and was pleased with excellent comments. The next morning I didn't feel splendid but put it down to strain. The day was Friday. On Monday we went to Glasgow. On Tuesday I sang *Schöne Müllerin*. On Wednesday, with the beginnings of a serious cold, I had two masterclasses. (All these for my old friend Philip Ledger.) Thursday I awoke with burning tennis-balls in my throat, rang up Munich and immediately cancelled the next show. I sang the second recital (Schumann and Rachmaninov) beautifully but in sheer agony. There is a time before a cold grips you with its flaming hands when you sing better than ever. Ask any singer and prove me right. I was told that no one else was possible for München. We took a plane from Scotland to London. Here I must stop because the pain of indecision is now too great, or perhaps the hurt of lassitude is too severe. Only now can I rely on totally natural reaction. Sleep is demanded. This is a constant. When breath becomes short, I sleep. This is a constant. I go to Munich. I try in vain to cancel. I must go on. I make a final move to stay my hysteria. I am now full of antibiotics and Fisherman's Friends. Half an hour to my entrance comes without breath. I must nail this. I ask my dresser to bring me a cup of tea. I go on. I sing. I sing well. It worked. But perhaps it would not have worked had I had a true physical cold. The next . . . Oh, let's forget the next. The problem with my neurosis is that

— — —

it seems to take its nourishment from so many different sources. One is duty. This is a concept which flies in the face of all that I believe. I wish to please. Why do I wish to please so unduly? Do I not love myself enough? I am greedy? The answer lies with all these less than admirable things. The real answer however, seems to be that I wish to control too much. I wish to dominate the situation and myself. This is impossible and being so breeds neurosis which in its turn robs me of (in this case) ten days of actual life and, because of the strain, possibly of years.

38

One of my greatest pleasures has always been visual art, paintings to be precise. In about 1970 I began to take a special interest in English drawings and watercolours and I suppose inevitably (because of my temperament) I was drawn to the more mystical pantheistic artists. I have always had particular love for Cozens with his ever-so-sad vision in blues and greens, death walks so obviously in all his pictures, his strange perspectives cloaked in memories of forgotten times and hopeless-ness. He is all tragic poetry. Thomas Girtin too, that poor fellow who died so tragically young and who with Turner transformed the old topographical traditions of the eighteenth century into something personal. In his work too I feel huge sadness but also complete acceptance. Again his palette was severely restricted. He painted in browns, greys, blues. He almost has a Dutch feel. Then my idol, Samuel Palmer. I love him not only for his much-praised Shoreham visions but also for the Milton and Vergil visions of his late life. I think his final watercolours and etchings sum up a creative life almost as *Falstaff* is the true expression of all that Verdi believed and learned. I admire John Martin, that man who out de Mille-ed de Mille before de Mille was born. Edward Lear I believe was one of the most truly religious artists. His landscapes speak of complete love of God and acceptance of his own sometimes miserable lot. But above all I love Blake. His vision, energy, mind, colour, madness, can fill me with wonder and stimulate in me thoughts for days and days. As Fuseli said, 'Blake is a great man to borrow from.' I could not agree more.

This unbidden resumé of my favourite English artists serves to lead me to a theory I have. This I should like to share with you. Shoot it out of the sky if you like. But do listen. (One small bit of privy intelligence: I prefer pictures which have an internal feeling, let me not call it a message lest I look even more foolish, to those which are about paint. How an artist puts his paint on is his affair and can be ravishingly beautiful, but give me a man that sees that which cannot be seen. Why paint something you can see?)

39

It was on one of my frequent sallies to Paris that I bought a book at the airport shop called *The Holy Blood and the Holy Grail*; it was by three people (Michael Baugent, Richard Leigh, Henry Lincoln), and fat, and clearly a bestest seller. Its burden, or tenor as I prefer to call it, was that Christ had married Mary Magdalene at the wedding at Canaan. It was their wedding. It was a dynastic wedding between the King of the Jews and a princess of a ruling tribe. The authors saw no irony or even sarcasm in the title Rex Judaeorum and there is no reason why they should, except that perhaps the Council of Nicaea had willed it. Mary had conceived a child which was de facto the son of God. When Christ's time came and he was crucified, the child with his mother Mary had taken a boat west to South-West France. (Another tradition tells us that Herod and Herodias were also to end their lives in this area.) This book implied that there was at the time, and possibly also now, a Holy Blood-line existing in France.

The argument is this. Potently armed with this knowledge, an arcane group has arisen. They had called themselves the 'Prieuré de Sion'. (This society still exists and has numbered among its grand masters, since its inception, Leonardo da Vinci, Victor Hugo, Debussy and Cocteau, to mention the stars.) In its turn and as a political wing, this Prieuré spawned the Knights Templar. Its brief was to find the written evidence pertaining to their knowledge. The actuality of the fact was said to lie in King Solomon's stables in Jerusalem. The knights undertook the mission, secured the documents and returned to France. The documents were finally secreted in Rennes-le-Château. This is a theory which is far from being secret. The Germans, in order to find the treasure, dug deeply into the soil of Rennes and found nothing. However, the Roman Catholic Church seems in some way to be ambiguous about Rennes, the parish priest for instance having more influence than seems natural for his position.

Now the interesting part begins and in no way rests upon the validity or not of the theory mentioned; the idea was enough to spark my imagination. I made a completely free association of thought. It was engendered by the book and will or will not stand whether the book is gnostic or not.

As secrets are notoriously hard to keep, so was this one. So many people were party to the intelligence that the secret would out. The Albigenses and others rioted against Rome and in the North various 'legends' suddenly appeared. The South-Western

French with their typical bureaucratic and pragmatic thought immediately accepted this truth and, as I previously mentioned, concealed it. On the other hand, the Germans and Northern Europe (without the actual documents) on hearing of the son of Christ, returned to what they knew of the crucifixion which was that among all the well-known incidents there was one in which Mary Magdalene took a cup and caught the drops of blood flowing from Jesus. In her cup or vessel or grail she held the blood, the very blood of Christ. The French had the real blood, still flowing; the Germans the symbolic blood. Out of the Teutonic tradition sprang the Holy Grail, Lancelot, Parsifal, Arthur.

The main symbol of the Prieuré de Sion was a broken pillar. After the political wing of the Prieuré had been formed there occurred the most horrendous schism between them. Both wished to be the absolute Sanctum Sanctorum of their truth. This schism was evidently symbolised by (because the fight occurred in high hot summer) a bolt of lightning shooting from a blue heaven, and cleaving an oak in two. At this moment my brain began to patter into action and formed its own hypothesis.

I had always been fascinated by Giorgione's painting 'La Tempesta', and have never been satisfied with the many and various explanations as to its meaning. Now I think I know. My theory won't convince the sometimes dull and oftentimes time-serving academics that are the heads of our institutions, but it might well amuse those who do not demand footnotes for their fun.

What I think I have found places the picture firmly in the iconographic school. No more mystery is left here, indeed no more mysticism. No more of the sexuality that Kenneth Clark tried to introduce, seeing a naked girl with baby, a man, and a broken pillar. Instead, a set of clear symbols intended for the arcane group who would recognise them. It is as if Giorgione is saying to the esoteric few, 'I know too, isn't it wonderful, but USHAP youra moutha.'

The pillar is the symbol of the Prieuré de Sion, the lightning flash the schism that rent its relationship with its spawning, the Templars. The naked girl is Mary Magdalene holding Christ's child in her arms. On the left is represented the northern tradition in the person of the knight holding the spear of ash (Wotan's symbol of life) in his hand. No doubt there are many arguments to be raised concerning this theory. However, it was painted in a symbolic age and probably for the delight or instruction of an elite. (Compare Botticelli, Fra Angelica and Elizabethan artists in their symbolic and esoteric work.) Anyway this idea literally came to me in a flash and has amused me, and I'm sure bored others greatly.

40

Here is fine advice from the best tenor so far, Caruso.

'It may be well to speak now of a very important point in singing – what is called the "attack" of the tone. In general this may be described as the relative position of the throat and tongue and the quality of voice as the tone is begun. The most serious fault of many singers is that they attack the tone either from the chest or the throat. Even with robust health the finest voice cannot resist this. This is the reason one sees so many artists who have made a brilliant debut disappear from sight very soon or wind up later on a mediocre career. Singers who use their voices properly should be at the height of their talents at forty-five and keep their voices in full strength and virility up to at least fifty. At this latter age, or close after it, it would seem well to have earned the right to close one's career.

'A great artist ought to have the dignity to say

farewell to his public when still in full possession of his powers, and never let the world apprise him of his falling-off.

'To have the attack true and pure one must consciously try to open the throat not only in front, but from behind, for the throat is the door through which the voice must pass, and if it is not sufficiently open it is useless to attempt to get out a full, round tone; also the throat is the outlet and inlet for breath, and if it is closed the voice will seek other channels or return quenched within.

'It must not be imagined that to open the mouth wide will do the same for the throat. If one is well versed in the art, one can open the throat perfectly without a perceptible opening of the mouth merely by the power of respiration. It is necessary to open the sides of the mouth, at the same time dropping the chin well, to obtain a good throat opening. In taking higher notes of course, one must open the mouth a little wider, but for the most part the position of the mouth is that assumed when smiling. It is a good idea to practise opening the throat before a mirror and try to see the palate, as when you show your throat to a doctor.

'In pronouncing the sound "ah" one must always attack it in the back of the throat, taking care, however, before uttering the syllable, to have the throat well open; otherwise what is called the "stroke of the glottis" occurs and the tone is hard and disagreeable. If you ever hear this stroke of the glottis on the attack, you may know that the singer did not attack far enough back in the throat.

'The tone once launched, one must think how it may be properly sustained, and this is where the art of breathing is most concerned. The lungs, in the first place, should be thoroughly filled. A tone begun with only half-filled lungs loses half its authority and is very apt to be false in pitch. To take a full breath properly, the chest must be raised at the same moment that the abdomen sinks in. Then with the gradual expulsion of the breath a contrary movement takes place. The diaphragm and elastic tissue surrounding and containing the stomach and vital organs, and the surrounding muscles by practice acquire great strength and assist considerably in this process of respiration, and are vital factors in the matter of controlling the supply which supports the tone. The diaphragm is really like a pair of bellows and serves exactly the same purpose. It is this ability to take in an adequate supply of breath and to retain it until required that makes or, by contrary, mars all singing. A singer with a perfect sense of pitch and all the good intentions possible will often sing off the key and bring forth a tone with no vitality to it, distressing to hear, simply for lack of breath control.

'This art of respiration once acquired, the student has gone a considerable step on the road to Parnassus. To practise deep breathing effectively it is an excellent plan to breathe through the nose, which aids in keeping the confined breath from escaping too soon. The nose also warms and filters the air, making it much more agreeable to the lungs than if taken directly through the mouth. In the practice of slow breathing make sure that the lungs are as nearly emptied as possible on the expulsion of breath before beginning a new inspiration, as this gives extra impetus to the fresh supply of air and strengthens all the breathing muscles.

'If this is not done, moreover, the effect is like two people trying to get in and out of the same narrow door at the same time.'

41

A may-fly salutes an eternal god and will stay silent. He also remembers hysterically funny times in his Aldeburgh seconds, and while he sits teeteringly happy in this possible last, would like to acquaint you of some.

In those old old days I remember, vaguely I admit, Ben Britten telling me that Peter had a terrible memory.

This was to be made startlingly clear. At Orford one night when we were about to perform *The Burning Fiery Furnace*, Nebuchadnezzar having some time to stew before his first entry, I heard a panicked but pathetic voice over my right shoulder. It was Peter, dressed in his orange and gold gear. 'Prompt, Bob. What are the words?' I was fairly amused as he had not yet started and said, 'Adept, Peter, Adept.' The line which was 'adept in magic' had clearly escaped his memory. He questioned me further, ever more urgently. 'Adept what, Bob, adept what?' I whispered, 'in magic,' and he was away.

I remember with razor memory a scene which happened in the Westerkirche in Amsterdam. The English Opera Group, or the Tooley Tours as it was known, was performing *Curlew River* at the Holland Festival. I was covering or understudying Peter. I took my seat in the body of the chancel, in some clerical worthy's seat, the snakes on the misericord looking marvellously virulent, and awaited the performance. Peter got into his first monologue, or rather began the music, for there was not a distinguishable word to be heard. There were many consonants finally and confidently delivered, but not one word. I heard: 'I come ... the ...w... ... ...ST. And ... . to the ST.' When the show was over I went to him to congratulate him and was met with, in that unmistakable high nasal voice almost exactly like mine, 'Oh, Bob, I had a slight lapse of memory tonight.' Lucifer had resumed his seat in Heaven. That brings me to a little unkindness that was visited on me at Orford in the same place. At my first performance, we waited to be congratulated by the duumvirate. Ben came first and was sweet, casting however a weather eye over his shoulder. Peter followed-on closely. He said to John Shirley Quirk, 'Absolutely stunning, John'; to Bryan Drake, 'Bravo, Bryan, well done'; and to me, 'Lipstick a little too white, I feel.' I was bemused but at that time too green to understand.

One of the most glorious moments of the Aldeburgh years happened in the final rehearsals of *Curlew River*. I was watching as understudy, sitting by Ben. The costumes had arrived and people were getting used to them: at least, most people were. Peter on the other hand was having a most distressing time with his dress (remember he was playing a woman). He would make his entrance with yards of thigh showing, then he would try it again and stumble on and end up with it over his head. Quite vexed, he brought the rehearsal to an end, saying, 'Really, Ben, I just can't work with this frock.' To which Ben replied to Colin Graham (producer), 'Oh, for Christ's sake, Colin, give her a crin.'

In the church operas we changed from monks into our characters in a sort of rugby scrum ruck. At one performance in Montreal I never managed to get my costume on. I had put my head through the armhole and was restricted so much in movement that I looked like the cliché-ed Arab selling dirty postcards, creeping round half bent with a devious look in one eye and panic in the other. All the performance I was encumbered thus. The orchestra, my colleagues, were doubled up. Ben in the audience could hardly believe his eyes. Peter, however, noticed absolutely nothing, showing complete bewilderment when told later of the hysteria.

Another fine moment happened in the Arts Theatre in Cambridge. I was not singing but watching from the wings. The piece this time was the *Rape of Lucretia*, a work with perhaps the worst libretto in the history of opera. At the end of the first act, all the guests at Lucretia's house line up to wish her goodnight. The students at Cambridge are notoriously cynical listeners. I remember going to the flicks there. Half the film was obliterated by the gusts of vacuous laughter which would erupt when a dubious line was uttered or a *double entendre* spotted. The first Good Night went well; the second, the audience was ominously quiet, the third brought the suspicion of a vicious titter. The fourth built quickly. The fifth, a gale of laughter rippled through the auditorium. The last, the roof nearly came off. Ben, conducting, was not amused. The male chorus has a frightfully difficult line to sing in the ride to Rome. 'Blood pouring from its hocks' has an obstinate way of sounding 'Blood pouring from its socks'.

Talking of words, Peter was notoriously bad at memorising them. He used to prepare an almost-new libretto in his mind for fear that he should forget the

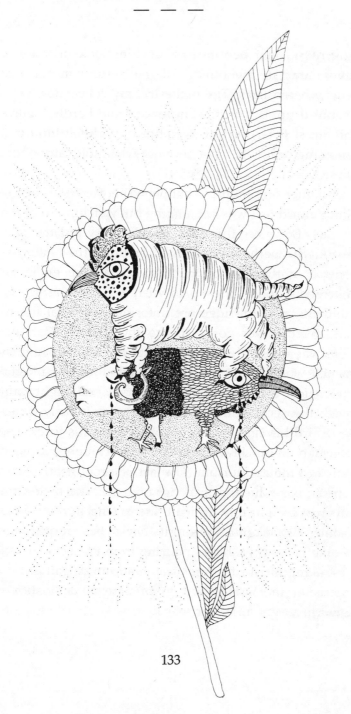

first. Consequently he had an alternative for almost everything. In *Curlew River* again there is a line that the Madwoman sings which goes, 'I have come to a tomb'. Peter being dubious about tomb creates grave as his alternative. Consequently we had at least two performances with the following: 'I have come to a toove' and better, 'I have come to a groom'. 'I have heard him singing in his grave' was often rendered, 'I have heard him singing in his bath'.

But above all it was in the rehearsals for the television recording of *Billy Budd* that the best Peterism happened. One of the finest theatrical moments in the opera occurs when the whole crew of the *Indomitable* prepare for battle against the Frenchman. The activity and excitement grows, they fire a cannon, the shot falls short, they prepare for another, then suddenly a mist descends. Then Captain Vere, speaking metaphorically concerning his inner struggle and actually concerning the mist, has to sing to a top B flat and back to F, 'O this cursed mist'. Peter, as was his wont, had decided that fog was probably a more effective word for the emotional moment. We received a gem. 'O this cursed fist' followed at the next run-through – possibly on purpose I have to admit – 'O this cursed mog'. All in all, and although I speak critically of the waspishness of the Aldeburgh days, I had never laughed for so long or so genuinely. The company was wonderful and the tours around Europe doing the church operas almost always a total hoot.

42

'Now rise up all the city and join our gallant army by noble Essex, Essex led.' My first utterings on the operatic boards were such. I was a young Welsh urchin, singing, or at least yelling, with the Covent Garden opera company which was touring with *Gloriana* in Coronation Year. The local youth had been dragooned into being singing extras. I mention this because it now draws my attention to the nature of success in singing and its dependency on a political Nous. As I mentioned previously, Colin Davis said that success was (and I paraphrase him) the ability still to be there, in other words when work stops so do you. I make this connection with *Gloriana* when I think of those Elizabethan characters closely assembled around and waiting on the power of the throne. When I consider Essex, I am appalled at his lack of political judgement, pride I suppose was his weakness, but his bull-headed pursuit of his own demise was remarkable indeed. Cecil did nothing, yet outlasted them all, Essex, Raleigh, Bacon and the Queen.

How much intelligence can we gather from this to use or filter into our experience? If 'still to be there' is the goal, and it certainly is my professional desire, then I think we must be confidently aware of where the power lies, but we should positively try not to be part of that power. A politically powerful base is defended with open claws and bared teeth. Trespassers are not prosecuted, but eaten. Thus we have a certain influence but no power of control.

43

It was interesting on two counts at least to revisit Aldeburgh again last year after fifteen years in exile. My final break with Ben occurred when both he and Michael offered me a part in their new operas. As Michael's was *The Knot Garden* and was to be given its premiere at Covent Garden, and as I liked Michael far the better at this time, I accepted the role of Dov and simultaneously sinned against the ghost and was dismissed from celestial Suffolk, with few fond farewells.

The roads which twenty years earlier were merely inadequate but promised stimulating endings were now battlefields. The juggernaut dared the world and the world was frightened. The roads were now too thin, too sectioned and hysterical (I do not drive). On leaving these runnels of horror the expected faery (sniggerers desist), unworldly, incestuous, ear-ringed world which accosted one then, no longer does. Where the birds once flew with a strange malevolence, they now just fly. Where the Forestry Commission plantations once held phantoms and northern dryads, they are now just proto paper. This depoetising of the countryside does not carry into the areas of Aldeburgh and Snape.

Having said with certainty that my zoo would not reassemble, I am now uncomfortably aware of claws on my left shoulder and a beak pecking ever so gently at my philosophical balance. It leaves as quickly as it came but is an uncomfortable souvenir of time spent. Aldeburgh itself is not now an obvious part of the Festival (probably good for the locals but pretty tedious for me). There is the ubiquitous deadly over-tutored watercolour exhibition – all contemporary de Wints without the powerful ugliness and character of the real thing – still in the estate agents. The print dress still orders mimsily in the necro-parlours of the hotels, unaware of any area of the under-used body it covers. The Moot Hall now looks 'craft tarty'. Apart from the odd blue plaque nothing of the duo, or indeed of music. In those old days, when reverence marks were at a premium, there was always the chance of a surprise. Perhaps an unsuspecting finger would be up a nose or a bum being satisfyingly scratched when around a corner would come the progress. There would appear Pope, King, a couple of sycophantic academics and perhaps a handmaiden or two strewing palms. It is indeed curious how such memories etch their spirit into sheer brick.

In Snape a different story unfolds. The over-resonant, once-useful building still reeks of the founders. There is built into the brick with semi-circular top, to the left of the stage and the right of the audience a kind of enormous bread oven. Ben, Peter and the directors took this as their royal box with its vantage view. From the stage it looked as if Beelzebub and his cronies were heatedly in recruitment. For me Snape heaves with unhappy memories.

44

I had come to Aldeburgh this time to sing with Julian Bream. His concerts I enjoy greatly. I only sing with him once every two years or so and after the comparative clarity of Wagner, Beethoven, Berlioz, even of Bach and Mozart, I find myself in the extremely ambiguous world of the Elizabethans. It is a peculiar relief to me. For this seemingly pure simple music is devoid of emotional clarity. Even a masterpiece like Thomas Morley's 'I saw my lady weeping' is emotionally and poetically so highly wrought that it is in some way suspect. Each gesture conceals a gesture and every word a word, and each irony a double irony. Yet the effect of this strange artificiality (a feeling I feel is equally shared by Manley Hopkins and Dylan Thomas, a sort of love affair with the building of words which in many ways precludes truth of expression) is to stimulate the mind forcibly. 'What is the exact emotion that I must find to express this piece?' 'How exaggerated can I be with its exaggeration?' But underlying all these fascinating quibbles of intent, there rests an earthiness and a grubby sexiness which has undeniable charm.

Working with Julian is an exciting high tension exercise. He is scrupulous and obsessive and a genius of his instruments. His reaction to music is to my ears invariably correct. Singing with him however poses very different technical problems. Most of the music I sing is either from the nineteenth or twentieth centuries. Between Dowland and Stravinsky comes, among thousands of others, Wagner. With his coming the concept, or at least the technique, of singing changed dramatically. Orchestras became not only larger but thicker, instruments were invented and included most of which performed in the middle ranges of the orchestra, adding to its weight. Concert and opera auditoria became vast to accommodate the increasing number of afficionados. The voice needed to become larger also in order to be heard at the back of these buildings. This inexorable growth of the voice is the antithesis of the instrument needed for Elizabethan songs. There is a certain level of body tension and volume needed in order to express the music through the self exactly. If this tension cannot be applied to a piece, then it must be similar to playing a violin on rubber bands. This tension cannot be applied in lute songs because of the weaker sound of the lute. Therefore I am left trying to improvise a new tension in order to apply the opposite intensity to the song. If I manage this by scaling down intensity of body and singing through a smaller aperture I am still faced by the words. 'Ah, fool; with that the nymph set up a laughing and blushed'. 'And blushed' now becomes the moving centre of the still world. How coy, how much blush? I presume to blush or would it be too much? The voice as an instrument of true meaning is now not in contention, but the songs demand their satisfaction and even with the feeling that the arsch-lock is near the glottis, they will get it, for they are great creations.

45

A beat of wings, a whistling of feathers tells me I am alone and inside again. My imagination is such a master, it calls and I career into myself to retreat and discuss. I am at a loss to explain the need for animals to attend me when I am in bitchy flood against human-ity. Thinking further I suppose that I need creatures to negate the anger I feel at man's arrogance.

I do envy the animal condition. If you start from my philosophical religious standpoint you will realise that all the areas of the intellect are not only of insignificance, but fraudulent. The intellect does not allow you to partake in the Godhead. It inhibits natural action with the question of meaning. Why and why again is the tenor (or perhaps I should say burden) of the intellect. What is why? It is in my view the trembling, perilous question of the dispossessed. It is a desire of the insecure. It is the playground of the loutish ego. It will ask with fashioned, burnished, invulnerable sentences; 'Why were we born? Why did this happen? Why do we die?' The answers which echo from the shell to deafen us are; Because we were, because it did, because we do.

The animals are too sharp to enquire in such a way. They seek scents, they love inordinately, they enjoy their food as much as we enjoy ours, I'm sure. When they are asleep they sleep, when awake suddenly, madly awake. Their noses sniff their gods, their loins tattoo in easy conscience. To be of that immediacy makes the second incandescent and makes me doubt all thought except that which says immediately before it that was good, that was very good, that was Good, that was God. These delicious feelings spring from that bit of us which knows without analysis.

Thought is but the looney breeze
That blows on schisty slates of carelessness
And hopes to change them.

Thought is but the bagatelle
That seeks to charm the blind-deaf God
And hopes for power.

Thought is but the selfish fear
That rails at death and hopes to confuse
Fate dozing in the egg.

46

Listening to a rehearsal not so long ago at the Festspiel-
haus in Salzburg, I had a revelation of what self-
perceived greatness can do to great music. The effects
are fundamental, almost producing catatonia. The
singers have been hired for their various abilities, the
most obvious being, to fill Mozart's notes with immediate life through soul and voice. Here I saw the conductor forbidding sound, thereby rendering the presence
of the singers superfluous. They were obviously filled
with awe or fear. When the rehearsals stopped and a
reference point was needed for starting again, each was
so in fear that the question of where they were going to

start could not be asked and so each stumbled along trying to get in by ear.

What I saw was the effect of ego allowed to flourish without pruning. More and more soil is sieved, fed, and watered, then a touch more bedding is added until the plant grows, flourishes and becomes so beautiful that it has no more relevance even for itself. It grows even higher, shuts its eyes and begins to perceive the world surrounding it as an irrelevance. The joys and pains and all bits of life become needless. The ego thus becomes not only divorced but ultimately irrelevant itself. I heard a performance of the opera as a mutilated symphony with voices; the only point of reference for me now being the arid notes so becomingly placed and so totally misunderstood.

47

It is for some time that I have felt the need to say something about the rather dubious area of recorded music. I use 'dubious' because most collectors of classical recordings have accepted the idea of the record as being not only an honest encapsulation of an event, but also as a valuable document of the time. I will ignore the various methods of storing these aural images (CD or not CD, DAT is the question) simply because it has no relevance for this performer. Two things I believe however do have importance. The first is practical and fundamental, the second philosophical but no less important.

When I walk into a studio (which in the past I did monotonously, but gladly far less now) I put myself totally into the hands of an enthusiast. This sounds offensive and of course is only meant to be provocative. I have spent years of learning technically how to sing, also how to think about music, how to read the drama, and how to show the passions which might easily be classified as love. I must work in this particular studio, because my contract says so.

I am greeted by the above enthusiast. He can be an amateur pianist, sometimes poet, a bit of a composer, perhaps even a bourgeois technocrat. However politically astute or even simply nice this person is, I am forced into a position of committing this offering of mine (however flawed) into his hands. I should like his power for he is a god. He will decide the balance, how strongly the flute comes through, the general orchestral sound, the brightness or darkness of sound, the closeness of the soloist, the joins between takes, the ambience and all areas of the musical feeling. This man is more important than all the assembled musicians and occupies the ground only just under the composer, thus the Decca recording of the *Ring* is not Wagner's *Ring* or even Solti's but Culshaw's. Now these record producers who cannot demonstrate a performing skill

are naturally little trusted by the bullets and sweat bri-
gade known affectionately as performers.

In the studio I am dealing with a critic (and I
have already discussed this condition) who decides
almost unilaterally and simply out of his taste what I
should sound like. It seems that one must achieve the
eminence of a performer like von Karajan before one
can order one's own destiny. It seems ironic that by
default I have to commit my passions to words or paint
(at both of which I have no particular gift) in order to
be understood, whereas that at which I am competent
is rendered vague by outside interference.

The second point is obvious when you think about
it but also interesting, and arises from a conversation
I had with Hockney. He surprised me when he said
that he thought the camera could only lie, the 'frozen
truth' being merely the passage of one truth to another
and the blurred image between being no truth either.
His thesis was, as I read it, that the nature of life is one
of constant flow and that as every second is moving
into the next until death, any isolation of a second or
a choosing of an attitude within one of these moments
is of itself false. The only truth of the motion of a life is
the life within the motion and not divorced from it by a
selective eye. In order to prove the lie of the camera he
had built up many frozen images as part of a whole into
large photographic creations. These have, by chance,
feelings of cubism but are more nearly concerned with
the breaking-down of the image, say a chair, into a

chair constantly changing with the flow of time.

The analogy between the photograph and the record is too close to be ignored. When I recorded '*Auf dem Strom*' of Schubert, it was from a young man in the instant, in the process of change, recorded by a young man in a similar condition and produced in a similar way. A million recordings of one bar would not produce a true reflection, because there could be no revisiting of a moment. (This is why memory too is such a liar, it being altered in our change.) Listening to one bar from five minutes on would make it a totally different one from that recorded or heard. What can be, and therefore what is, is a compromise and an enabling of heinous proportion which masquerades as a 'statement' of truth. I will not excuse my fellow artists from this acidic gripe. When I see a tenor who will not sing above F when the recording panoply is around him, i.e. orchestra, conductor, fellow singers, but will studiously and stubbornly pipe it in note by note at a later date, I would ask the public to guard its purse. Those who have seen clearly the incipient lie of recorded music have always done it best.

48

I was looking into a meat shop in Salzburg not so long ago, when I was pulled out of my thoughts by Lucia Popp. I said, 'Lutzi, how are you?' She answered, 'I feel like a piece of furniture, what else?' I asked her why and she told me that she was rehearsing *Capriccio*. This hanging-around and being moved – no, pushed – around is one of the more tedious bits of a singer's life. However, it is quite gratifying to know that we have the last word, at least.

As I walk around Salzburg I see huge photographs of conductors, pianists, singers, fiddlers looking at me from hoardings, and taxis, smaller ones from record covers and programmes. Some are macho, some winsome, some innocent boyish, some inscrutable, all hideous. I question the need for this idiotic personality cult. Do I really have to accept these crass ideas? Ideas of arrogance and money conceived by company and artist in equal culpability.

I would say to them, 'I could never be happy in these specious parameters.'

They would say to me, 'You were never good enough to deserve such recognition.'

I to them, 'Recognition peels me.'

Them to me, 'You never loved yourself enough to join.'

I, 'I loved myself too much to be interested.'

Them, 'You were too lazy to play our game.'

I, 'Yes.'

But when so many other games are available which leave me free of others' influence, why join the one in which I am marked for others' gain? This has always bemused me. If I do not believe the lie, why in heaven's name should I support those who do? I must never become *theirs*. This is crucial.

49

Before I bring these flighty fancies to a seeming end, I feel that I should say something about conducting. I am, as yet, a mere beginner in this arcane pursuit, having conducted to date no more than about forty concerts. However my ideas are beginning to form and I freely admit that I like it greatly.

For twenty-nine years I have sat as near to conductors as it is possible to be, and have seen real talent on very few occasions. The great conductors

can be measured on one hand and two or three fingers of the other. The rest can be categorised as the nasty and musical, the nice and musical (perhaps ten per cent or so) and the not musical at all – the very large remainder. Thinking most arrogantly that there might be a little more music, communication and dramatic imagination in me, I decided to try my arm.

At the start I found the idea of controlling eighty or so disparate egos, all of whom I respected greatly having been one of them for so long, not a little daunting. Gradually however, it became clearer and clearer that they were waiting to see themselves again, and to give them a clearer identity of their worth is, I think, my task. Each violinist is at the start of his playing entrusted with the spirit of music and self-expression, each is surely a 'Heifetz' to his mother, and because of this he soon visualises himself commanding the heights of Mendelssohn into the vacuum of the Albert Hall in a simple unstoppable step. This hardly ever happens, and before long the mother's gift finds himself at twenty-five or so in the back desk of a symphony orchestra or even trying (and now I'm being unduly cynical) to convince himself that he is playing a baroque fiddle not because he is more individual in a baroque band, but because he believes in authenticity. (By the way, after eleven years, the authentic *War Requiem* is gone – no one can do it now, except perhaps Jeffrey Tate, in the way that Ben would have recognised it, and this is the case even with a record to listen to. What hope have we with the

Missa Solemnis and all the rest of history?)

How is this deep disillusion coped with by our archetypal fiddler? He can and often does move into sullenness, if one can move into such a thing, approaching nihilism. The attitude can become a trifle hostile and he can become part of a musical assembly line. With many members of an orchestra feeling in a similar way, a collective shell can be created around the body by way of protection. Thus orchestras can develop a collective personality with which they protect themselves from hurt. However, in so doing they isolate themselves from joy and lightness of hours.

The conductor must pierce the collective shell. He can attempt this in two basic ways. Either he becomes a martinet, a 'real bastard' showing little consideration to the players, or he adopts an attitude of identification with the players in a kind of democratic approach.

I chose this second method (it being closest to my temperament). I first made the mistake of believing that all the musicians were replicas of me with strong musical ideas and a natural intolerance of authority. In this I was soon proved wrong and I understood that the players were waiting to be guided. This was no essay in democracy but rather an exercise in concealed authoritarianism. Once I realised this simple fact, joy, shared fun, could begin. It became my task to make them believe in their own musical gift, to stop interfering, to let them play, not to make corners where there were none and above all not to try and play their instruments for them. It really is amazing how many people will show wonderful colours of love when you don't hide from them. If you try and conceal yourself for a moment they will spot it and you will be consigned to the phony heap. But just for a second show your good, God good wonder-side and they will run open-hearted forward. Suddenly a three-hour session passes in seconds. I have an almost pathological loathing of rehearsals, believing that when the notes are more or less in place and the type of interpretation has been given to the band, then it is time to leave well alone and leave the rest to the inspiration of the moment. The conductor who over-rehearses has a distinct problem with his security, I believe. He attempts to control tomorrow from today; this is rubbish and succeeds only in blunting both players and spirits.

If asked to compare the difficulties of singing and conducting and to decide which was the easier I think I would have to say conducting. They are both difficult jobs, but the very fact of producing noise outweighs the brain-organisation of beats and mathematics. The emotional quality is almost identical. It is true also that a conductor works all the time while a singer sits and thinks on the platform, or drinks coffee and yarns in his dressing-room. But nothing is worse than that awful morning when you rise, feel those throaty hot spots and have to dare your technique yet again, and, at that time to wave goodbye to the high B with an arm suspiciously free (as yet) of arthritis and freezes, is wildly seductive.

50

The house with the troublesome number of rooms now calls me to attention once again, and I hope quite sincerely for the last time. I however from my deep experience doubt it. I am sitting warm in a conservatory surrounded by evil-smelling geraniums, the offspring of tree seeds pocketed in various parts of the world, and wicked cacti (I am always glad and sometimes even give praise that such plants can't walk), when I feel a knocking, or perhaps I smell something other than the flowers or even sense something more than the heat. Whatever this thing is, it is undeniable and drags me inexorably out of my sweaty damp world. I put on a pair of black velvet slippers with silver thread fish on them and begin, like some hound, to follow my sense.

First I sniff the air, take bearings and go left – yes, that's the way. This strange ribbon of sense is getting stronger. I leave the ground floor and begin to pass the rooms I have recently discovered, the ones with phosphorescent colours, those with 'questions only' marked on the doors, those with 'only answers', and the ones

I especially like with 'no questions or answers' clearly marked. In these last, I remember, is no movement and total unity of all creation: all creation wildly still, turbulently still. Onward I walk and upward and then, in a dark corner and I must confess in a place where I have never been before, I see the dusty beginning of a stone stair.

The ribbon is now almost tangible. I have no choice but to follow. I now see the sense-ribbon: it is yellow with occasional red bands, perhaps every yard, obviously a sort of marker. At first the staircase is wide, quite wide enough for a decent pair of shoulders, and I walk and climb with only the normal difficulty (caused in the left leg by ascending too many ladders in Turns of the Screw and in the right by a partial Achilles tendon loss).

There is something unnerving about this place. Why had I not known of it? Or is it after all *my* house? If this has lain undiscovered, how much more might there be? What if the rooms contain things that I don't want to admit, or even to know, what if my bliss were shattered? I put such impish thoughts away and decide that I will only seek when the sense tells me and the ribbon leads me.

Suddenly, but pianississississimo faint, I hear a sound. It is at first a gentle hum like that passacaglia you sometimes hear the Earth playing when God is your soul. It starts, I believe, way above, somewhere right at the top of this tower, for that is what the staircase is.

As the sound gets louder the staircase narrows until shoulders are near to the dusty, crusty, webby sides. I still climb, feeling that although the tower is becoming darker by the step, I am inevitably walking into the light. I hope this is so. The sound ahead is becoming more recognisable, it is forming itself into a low, perceptible sound of voices. The ribbon of sense is trembling slightly as if it is carrying the sound.

I have gone up now for about five minutes. I can almost make words of the sounds. I hear syllables, con ... con ... tion ... tion. Suddenly I can see where the sound is coming from, my ribbon leads straight to it. There is a small round hole in the inside wall. It is covered with a grill wonderfully wrought with Celtic symbols. Round the outside of the grill, carved in stone, figures of gryphons, grape leaves, dogs with horns, rams, oak leaves all entwine, twizzle together like a pit of mating snakes, sometimes a dog is a leaf sometimes a goat is a tree.

I look inside towards the sound and am struck near senseless by what I see. There in a huge room with no exterior light are thousands of people. The room looks like a religious building, it has the soul of the sacred about it. I can only just see to the end of it. It begins in what I will loosely call a Romanesque style and develops through Norman, Gothic, Perpendicular, Baroque, Rococo until today, which is nearest me. It is hard to make out much, for the room is full of scents (perhaps this is my ribbon all the time). Towards the middle of this chamber there shoots up high (rather like a weaver bird's nest) a twisting funnel of stone painted gold and silver in regular but diminishing diamonds. At the top of this funnel a small, a very small opening leads to the air and, from where I am standing, seems to have no glass cover. The people too seem to cover humanity's time, from the way they are dressed. Deep down, where the incense turns into blue smoke, I think I see people in skins. As with the architecture, so with the people: the closer to me the more modern the style they wear.

Time has assumed its natural way and stopped. The Heavens cease to spiral and reverse, my watch has stopped. I've been here for ever. I have seen everything, everything I knew without knowledge. But what a scene. All the thousands – no, millions – of people there are chained to a creation of man. Not so far from me thousands sit around a score of the St John Passion, and from their ankles and wrists I see powerful but beautiful wires leading to the score which is itself secured to the wall. Then I see a Memling tryptich, also fastened to the wall, and in front of it countless people similarly tethered. Far back, the people in skins are chained to an image of the sun. I see someone like me sitting before a Cecil Collins virgin, but he's not quite attached, the wires won't reach. There is a host of people near the score of Parsifal, all joined together and to the book by this same not painful, even comforting, but unbreakable wire.

— — —

The most remarkable thing was that all these willing prisoners appeared giddily happy. Each one smiled, some wept, all appeared in a state of grace. But I felt uneasy, especially as the one like me seemed unattached. I felt, my deep old soul told me, that something was amiss. I now gave an ear to the cry that went up as if from one throat, and the world was Consolation.

What was Consolation? The word implied for me separation. So I shouted through the grill, and caught somebody's gaze.

'Why do you chain yourself to an icon?'

'Because it frees me from loneliness.'

'Why bow before an image?'

'Because it makes me one with humanity.'

'Why do you cry Consolation?'

'Because I need consoling for my separation from God.'

'Why are you separate from God?'

At that moment the swirl and howl of noise became so intense that his answer was lost. But I was left thinking that this consolation through the image however holy, however of great report, however spiritual, was just in fact what I was seeing. It was a jailor, rather like all the other concepts that I had considered, but more subtle and more lethal. Sacred art was being used to keep man in his place. In a place separate from God.

And again I thought, what is Consolation? Why should it be necessary? How can you be consoled

157

from yourself? If you are God, or at least a part of God, as the begetter and the begotten must be the same, what separation can there be? There is no need for consolation from whatever lofty source. We are our own consolation. We are consolation. At that moment a bird flew over the hole in the funnel, and the scene went black.

51

Recently, I have accepted the Chair of International Vocal Studies at the Royal Academy of Music. My duties, apart from keeping a watchful eye over new talent, are to give various masterclasses.

Masterclasses are areas of immense control and power. Here I am faced by unformed souls, virginal, expectant, open. Here is dangerous ground for the hungry ego. Because of this, more self-control is needed than in any other of the musical theatres.

What do these innocents lack most? I suppose the concept of the shortness of time. They are terribly sweet and very complacent. Having little idea of mortality they saunter and laze both in mind and spirit. Death being such a stranger, there is little need to be involved in the passion of nowness, except perhaps corporeal couplings. This in turn means that they arrive

at my class but half-awake, half-prepared, dead in the
head and half-alive in the voice. They then rest their
lazy souls and perform constant cliché. Touching the
piano, pressing the hands together as if in continuous
prayer, vacantly addressing the moods and situations
of what they sing, vapidly scanning the audience,
trying to charm with head bobs, lip twists and shy
shimmies, they evade the bloody truths of the stories
of which they sing.

What do the naive lack most? Imagination, passion,
awareness and love are part of the answer. They conceal the basic self, hiding from possible embarrassment
and hurt in a shell of received interpretation. Perhaps
these qualities arrive later, like essence after bottling,
perhaps they don't rest in some souls. My task, and it
is hard physical and emotional work, believe me, is to
create in these pretty people possibilities, awarenesses.
I must force their unwilling bodies into real situations.
I must ignite the fuel of their imaginations.

All this is truly possible and the most amazing results
are suddenly upon you. Deep personal feelings are
liberated, the piano becomes white-hot with electric-
ity, it is untouchable. Limbs are suddenly freed. The
dull theatre turns a phosphorescent gold. The world
reverses on its axis. Next time most are back to the
crutches of cliché.

52

A last word on conducting. A story never to be forgotten by the arrogant novice.

'What is the difference between a bull and an orchestra?'

'With the bull the horns are at the front and the arse at the back.'

53

With my kind of temperament, one of fatalism and optimism in almost equal parts, it is not surprising that I have no regrets for myself. I would have wished perhaps to have lived at a less scientific time. I certainly would have wished to have been in a less political time, but that time has never been. I would have liked a world in which words were redundant and perceived love the only method of talk. I would hope for a Jungian

world where psychology and religion become comple-
mentary, where the historical spiritual leaders Christ,
Mohammet and Lao Tse, are seen not as special but
part of the archetypal ground from which we take our
deeply intuitive truths, where the sense of the mystery
and the numinous are alive and kicking in every soul.

I would also wish (illogically) for a rediscovery of
the lost gnostic gospels and a finding of the historical
Christ and the ability to rewrite Nicaea and a grand-
stand seat for viewing Pauline Christianity in all its
political pomp as it comes shrieking and falling from
the pinnacle of its own lies. I would wish that Mozart
could live every century and that Van Gogh would
paint my walls and that I had a dog's concentration in
the moment, that sniffed bright awareness of each and
every now; that real rest in tiredness. I would wish also
always to see and feel that similar joy and concentration
of my dear colleagues at work, Susanna singing birdily
alive, charming unduly and making the eyes water.

What is the singing, then? It is of such colossal
immediacy. Every second is a year, each minute eternity. In such sometimes, every sinew quivers as strings
tune and oboes forget the fields. Voices almost out
of ear, felt in the veins, the intense quick, Guten
Abend Professors, Good evening Sir Johns, darling
everybodies; Indian footmen, managers, sub-mana-
gers, sub sub sub librarians. Then listen to that quiet
and that strange uncommitted applause and then nose
that vibrating air and that Susanna again high kicking

161

and not making shadows, Figaro walking his clothes, impression on feeling, feeling on ears, ears on skull, a heavy curtain rises painfully fast and 'now' is long and instant.

I would wish at this joyful moment for eternal life with my best-friend-wife and daughters. I now deliberately have no ideas concerning eternity; however, my experience tells me that everything I construct as truth is almost certainly wrong. So I will wait and watch. Meanwhile, when I write another exercise of this kind and that will be, of course, at the end of the next fifty years, I will write it in chapters and headings and organise it in a way more generally approved of and in the way we were taught to conquer the Tripos. Tear here, is now going to do something more interesting.